PRAISE FO

"This poignant—yet hilarious—memoir tracks Frankel's lifelong battle with the scale—or, more accurately, with herself. As she diets through good times and bad, Frankel skewers her own weight-loss foibles and a society that teaches women that thin is all that matters."
—Lucy S. Danziger, editor-in-chief, *Self* magazine

"The rueful, zestful, surprisingly funny story of Ms. Frankel's battle reads like a sequel to the adventures of the chubby heroine of Judy Blume's young-adult novel *Blubber.*"　　　—*The New York Times*

"Val Frankel is a woman of amazing insight. . . . She takes the step all women who have had lifelong insecurities in front of the mirror must: to face them down and triumph over them. And the fact that she learned how to dress well along the way doesn't hurt either. Read this, weep, and heal."
—Stacy London, cohost of *What Not to Wear*

"I loved this book, as will anyone who's ever looked in a mirror and not always liked what they've seen. Val Frankel's tragicomic memoir of her battle of the bulge is alternately riotously funny and deeply poignant, but always thought provoking. And when ultimately her struggle ends up being less with her belly fat than with her own inner demons, it ends up being downright inspiring."
—Meg Cabot, author of The Princess Diaries
and Queen of Babble series

"[A] gritty, funny tale about one woman's quest to jettison a lifetime's worth of hang-ups, not to mention a closet full of Old Navy duds."
—*Entertainment Weekly*

"[F]unny and brutally frank . . . a satiating account of the long road to self-acceptance."   —*People* magazine

"Val Frankel's *Thin Is the New Happy* proves that coming to terms with one's body image might not be easy, but is definitely poignant and hilarious. I applaud Val Frankel's bravery and found myself compelled and inspired by her memoir. Doesn't matter what size you are—if you're a fan of a great story, *Thin Is the New Happy* is the perfect fit."   —Jen Lancaster, author of *Pretty in Plaid*

"Infused with humor and refreshing candor, the book will resonate with anyone who's counted carbs or tried to subsist on rice cakes and grapefruit . . . a self-aware, witty exploration of a woman's body issues."   —*Kirkus Reviews*

"[F]resh, insightful weight-loss memoir."   —*OK!* magazine

"I loved *Thin Is the New Happy*, a memoir by a very good, very funny writer about things that aren't funny; it made me laugh, it made me cry, and it made me think. Now I'm telling everybody I know to read it, too; women because we all struggle with body issues, and men so they'll know what we're up against."
                    —Jennifer Crusie, author of *Bet Me* and *Wild Ride*

"If you are what you weigh, read this book. Valerie Frankel's honest account of life on and off the scale is a victorious and funny account of the diet wars."   —Betsy Lerner, author of *Food and Loathing*

"[A] funny, smart memoir . . . inspiring in a totally down-to-earth way."   —*Parenting*

THIN

IS THE

NEW

HAPPY

THIN

IS THE

NEW

HAPPY

Valerie Frankel

🦁 ST. MARTIN'S GRIFFIN 🐙 NEW YORK

www.stmartins.com

The Library of Congress has catalogued
the hardcover edition as follows:

Frankel, Valerie.
    Thin is the new happy / Valerie Frankel.—1st ed.
        p. cm.
    ISBN 978-0-312-37392-4
   1. Frankel, Valerie.   2. Authors, American—20th century—
Biography.   3. Dieters—United States—Biography.   4. Weight loss—Psychological aspects.   5. Body image.   I. Title.
    PS3556.R3358Z46   2008
    813'.54—dc22
    [B]   2008020439

ISBN 978-0-312-37393-1 (trade paperback)

10 9 8 7 6 5

Dedicated to …
THE LAST FIFTEEN POUNDS

I don't miss you,
Not one tiny bit,
You bitches.

ACKNOWLEDGMENTS

So many people to thank, so few letters in the alphabet.

A lot of authors thank their husbands last. Screw that! Thank you, Steve! You're number-one for me, sweetie! My daughters, Maggie and Lucy, give me boatloads of inspiration and motivation. To quote Roger De Bris's solo in a fine musical by Franz Liebkind, "Everything I do, I do for you!"

I ask, where would any writer be without friends she could steal from and bitch to? For all the funny lines, home-cooked meals, snappy e-mails, emotional support, and brutal honesty, I have to thank/give credit to Rebecca Johnson, Judy McGuire, Nancy Jo Iacoi, Daryl Chen, Judith Newman, Liz Brous, Dana Isaacson, and Ann Billingsley.

My parents, Howie and Judy Frankel, take their hits on these pages. That hasn't stopped them from telling friends, acquaintances, and complete strangers on the street to buy the book. Their support has been unflagging. I can only hope to be as tireless a cheerleader to my kids as you both are for me. My sister, Alison Frankel, selflessly talked to me for *hours* during the writing process. She always asked the right questions and pointed my thoughts in the right direction. Just one more time in our lives that Alison helped me get here from there.

Articulate shrinks are a magazine writer's best friends. Ed Abramson and Joan Chrisler submitted to interviews and countless follow-ups, getting nothing in return for their time. They put me on the Not Dieting path, also, for which I can't be thankful enough.

Stacy London: You are incredible! What you did for me was beyond generous. I applaud and admire your determination to spread the joy of personal style, one wardrobe at a time.

My editor at St. Martin's, Jennifer Enderlin, has amazed me with her dedication and commitment. At times, I felt like this book was as important to her as it was to me. She laughs, she cries, she uses a lot of exclamation points (!!!) and CAPS in her e-mails (which I ADORE!!!). Jennifer is the Woody Allen of book editors. Every writer out there would drop anything, and would be honored, to work with her.

I owe a huge thanks to a handful of magazine editors as well. Several chapters started out as articles. Lucy Danziger, Dana Points, and Paula Derrow agreed to let me pose nude for an essay in *Self,* providing me with cocktail party fodder for the rest of my life. Susan Chumsky and Amy Gross hired me to write a piece about bad body image for *O* magazine that proved just how far down the rabbit hole I'd fallen. Without tasting the subject matter in small bites first, I doubt I'd have ever bellied up to the feast.

Nancy Yost, my agent, had represented me for nine years and ten novels when she suggested I try something different for a change. A year and a half later, my life, relationships, body, and thoughts *have* changed, dramatically, for the better. Whatever she tells me to do next, I'm there.

BEFORE

approached the scale. Small, slow steps. I pretended I was walking through water.

"Just get on there," said my mother impatiently.

Exhaling, as if pressing air out of my lungs would make me lighter, I climbed aboard. The numbered wheel spun.

"Oh. My. God," said Mom when the spinning stopped. Tears formed in her eyes; her chin quivered. Her disappointment couldn't have been deeper had I committed mass murder.

I had, instead, committed a serious nonviolent crime. I was chubby. Not fat, mind you. Not large enough to qualify for my own zip code. But I was decidedly big-boned. By 1976 Short Hills, New Jersey, standards, even medium-boned was offensive. My mom, a slim woman (by nature and neuroticism), said, "You're officially on a diet. And I'm going to make you stick to it—for your own sake. You'll thank me one day."

I wasn't feeling the gratitude that afternoon. While Mom

busied herself logging my current weight on her clipboard chart, I looked down at the number on the scale. I was in sixth grade, five feet tall with emerging boobs. I weighed 100 pounds. I'd hit three digits before puberty. Unthinkable! My small-boned sister, Alison, two grades older, hadn't yet crossed the line.

The impetus for Project Daughter Diet was our upcoming family vacation to the Club Med in Guadeloupe. My mom was not going to let me embarrass myself (or her), running around at a tropical resort, a chubby cherub in a bikini. She would spare me the humiliation, regardless of whether I knew I was feeling it. As of that first official weigh-in, my pudge became her heavy burden, one more responsibility she had to shoulder.

And she bore it mightily. Immediately, Mom's crackdown began. Daily calorie counts. Food rationing. Mom colluded with other adults, besides my dad, to monitor my intake. The mothers of my friends would serve me celery sticks after school while giving their own daughters cookies and milk. Teachers discouraged other kids from sharing the contents of their lunch boxes with me. At home, neither Ring Ding nor Twinkie passed between my lips. Crust was cut from Skippy and Wonder Bread sandwiches. Apples replaced chips. I cried, threw tantrums. I hated feeling picked on, scrutinized, deprived. But I couldn't deny that the diet was working. My Sunday weigh-ins proved that I was shedding pounds.

After six weeks, I approached the scale for the final pre-trip weigh-in. Tunnel-visioned, I watched the dial spin until it rested, the needle pointing to the number 88. I jumped into my mother's arms with elation. We hugged and cried big fat sloppy tears of joy.

I'd done it—gone below the goal of 90 pounds. As much as I'd loathed the process, I reveled in the result. I was sleeker, faster, lighter. My clothes hung on me instead of puckering around bulges. My face was bony, my eyes gigantic, like the bug-eyed waifs' on black-light posters. I both resented and soaked up the flattery from the adults who'd conspired against me. I smiled prettily in response to their praise while secretly wishing them dead. My sixth-grade teacher, a fat-assed fan of polyester pantsuits, pulled Mom aside at pickup and said, "Valerie looks fantastic! What a figure! How on earth did you *do* it?"

What a figure. I was eleven freaking years old.

Enforced dieting at that age can certainly skew one's perspective. I developed a premature and acute sense of cynicism. At the Club Med, I ran around in my bikini with the carefree detachment of a girl who didn't care about a number on the scale, fully aware of the cold irony that I'd been that girl two months earlier. Sizewise, I was on a par with my skinny sister and wiry younger brother, Jon. Mom watched me proudly from her beach chaise, pointing me out to the French and German vacationers in neighboring chairs, smiling smugly at what must have been their polite acknowledgment of my attractiveness. By dropping twelve pounds, I'd won the approval of my parents, their friends, teachers, complete strangers, everyone and no one whose opinion carried weight.

I was hooked. The approval was river wide, ocean deep. I became convinced of my own unparalleled beauty. The pounds that once hid my profound loveliness were gone, and now I shone like the sun. My fat-free body was bullet-proof, superstrong, a secret weapon I hadn't realized I possessed. Being thin made me happy. It made my mother happy.

But, sadly, the joy was fleeting. After the trip (I'd gorged on the omnipresent buffets), I stepped back on the scale and was stunned that I'd re-gained four pounds. *But, but, but . . . I am* thin *now,* I thought, as if it were a permanent condition. The blunt and sudden understanding—that if I wanted to continue to shine like the sun, to bask in praise and glory, I would have to eat celery sticks *forever*—gave me a physical pain in the gut. I looked heavenward and screamed, "Noooooo!!!"

The two sources of happiness in my childhood were at odds. I could have food. Or I could have approval. I couldn't have both.

It should come as no surprise to anyone that food won the day, the year, the decades. The quest for approval, however, endured. At age eleven, I became a chronic dieter. A brass ring grasper. A pie-in-the-sky eater. By the numbers, I'd tried approximately 150 distinct diets, every trendy one to come down the pike, as well as scores of my own invention. In my adult life, I'd been as small as a size six and as big as a fourteen. I'd lost and re-gained hundreds of pounds. Dropping weight always equaled victory, validation, the (re)claiming of my rightful status as pretty-on-the-outside. Gaining weight equaled failure, weakness, faulty character, a demo-

tion to really-good-personality. I'd been up and down the
diet road so many times in the last thirty years that my foot-
prints were potholes. Monuments dotted the roadside, mark-
ing my thinnest periods, my fattest, the ghastly pig-outs, the
incredible displays of self-control that appeared blurry as you
sped by.

By the way, you like dieting metaphors? Pull up a chair. I
could go all night.

A drug addiction. My initial success was like a first hit of
crack. Instantly addicting. A high I'd chase forever. I had a
chubby monkey on my back. I was hooked on dieting, always looking for the next fix, be it South Beach or French
Women. No matter how high (meaning thin) I got, I
craved more, never certain where my next hit was coming
from.

A gambling addiction. I kept trying to replicate that first big
win, but couldn't. I lost my shirt (but not my flab) in the process. The odds were stacked against me. To play, I stared
goggle-eyed at a spinning numbered wheel. Unless I hit 21
(pounds lost), the diet was a bust.

A sex addiction. One diet wasn't enough to satisfy me. I
needed to try another, and another, and none of them kept
me satisfied for long. The harder I tried to deny my lusts, the
more inflamed they became, until giving in to desire was all
I thought about. My insatiable appetite compelled me to
cheat, and cheat again.

Or how about *chronic dieting as psychiatrist Elisabeth Kübler-
Ross's five stages of grief*? Denial: "This diet is going to be the
one that works!" Anger: "Everyone *else* has cake." Bargain-
ing: "I cheated today, so I'll work out double tomorrow."

Depression: "I can't believe I ate the whole thing." Acceptance: "It's useless. I'll never be thin."

When I finally shuffle off this mortal coil, my tombstone should read: "Here lies Valerie Frankel. She dieted." I might go to my deathbed wishing I'd left a skinnier corpse.

I was gearing up to take my kids to Florida, to Disney World, where I expected to see a lot of people far fatter than me. It was a bathing-suit vacation. With the predictability of the setting moon, I put myself on a prevacation diet. It wasn't as easy to drop weight at forty-one as it was at eleven, but I had to try. I dreaded the appraisal of strangers, people who couldn't possibly care less how much flab spilled over the top of my bathing suit. I dieted for them anyway, like a conditioned lab rat. As I chopped my pretrip lettuce lunch, I imagined I was starring in an absurdist drama that I wrote for myself. Absurd, and ridiculously long. How would my weight obsession end? *Would* it ever end? Would I *really* take my weight obsession to the grave? Scarier still, would it live on after I was gone in future generations?

My mother's fatphobia was instilled in her by my appearance-obsessed grandmother. A vain alcoholic, anorexic narcissist and spoiled housewife with an evil streak, Fay was a true sadist. Nothing amused her more than making Judy—her daughter, my mother—cry and grovel in genuine fear for her safety. As a mother herself, Judy at her worst was a cream puff in comparison to Fay. My grandmother passed down her obsession with looks to Judy. Judy passed down body anxiety to me. It was in my genes, wormed under my skin so deeply it was as much a part of me as the skin itself.

My daughter Maggie was a sixth grader, eleven years old, the age when it all began for me. Lithe and limber, Maggie was spared what Alison and I called "the struggle." Then again, Maggie could thicken up. One never knew what adolescence might bring. She came home from school with stories about the fat girls in her class, kids whose lifelong battles were just beginning. Boys teased them, oinked and mooed behind their backs, asked them out only to laugh in their face when they said yes. When I saw these girls at school, my heart would break for them. I was teased in middle school. I felt their pain. If any boys ever teased Maggie, I'd do to them what I would have loved to do to my adolescent tormentors: corner them, unleash the power of my superior weight, kick the living crap out of them, give them the punishment they deserved.

My younger daughter, Lucy, eight and in second grade, had stretched three inches ever the summer. Formerly soft and round, she became lean and ropy seemingly overnight. The first day back to school, a few mothers at drop-off noticed the change. They cooed over her scrawny legs and sharp collarbone and gave her the "what a figure" treatment. Lucy soaked up compliments with the same greedy lust I had. Never vain before, Lucy started spending hours in front of the mirror. She rambled on and on about "how great it is to be skinny." I disgusted myself by admiring her visible ribs, hoping this wasn't a temporary taste of slimness that she'd hunger for forever.

I didn't tell Lucy my thoughts or compliment her new shape. Before I had daughters—before I'd menstruated, before I'd *heard* of menstruation—I vowed that I'd never harass my future children about their weight. I wouldn't do to them what my mother did to me (what her mother did to her, and so on, and so on). Much as I tried to impart the healthy attitude, the "love yourself for who you are" message, my daughters weren't fooled. They had eyes and ears. They saw and heard what I put myself through: my dieting cycles, anxiety about food, dread of bathing-suit vacations, rising and falling and rising weight. I was a bad example.

Weight anxiety had had me in its grip for thirty years. When I looked at Maggie and her friends and realized how young they were, I was amazed and saddened that I'd been introduced to self-loathing at their age. I mourned for the wasting of my wonder years, the abandon I missed, how lonely I must have been. All the years and hours wasted since then. I wasn't blaming anyone. My problem with body image was my responsibility. As Oprah would say, I owned it. I'd owned it for years. But now, at the age of forty-one, I'd wanted to disown it.

My journey out of the waistland would require confrontations, unlearning, mind sweeping, and cleaning skeletons—and clothing—out of my closet that didn't fit the woman I wished to be. Coming to terms with my diet demons seemed more doable than losing twenty pounds, actually. More worthwhile, too, given what was at stake.

Even more than love, I wished for my daughters a life of comfort in their skin. I had to break our family tradition, ensure that Maggie and Lucy felt superstrong and bullet-proof, no matter what their shape. I had to show them how, but first I would have to figure it out. For me, the struggle started with my mother. For my daughters, the struggle would end with me.

1

DIETS ARE FOREVER

Hello, my name is Val, and I'm a diet addict. I exist on a continuous loop of starting a diet, recovering from one, and planning the next. I'm either counting calories, fat grams, carbs, or the number of days until I begin anew (and it's always "for the last time"). Dieting defines me. It grounds me. If I didn't have a diet to plan or follow, I'd panic. Going cold turkey on dieting would be a shock to my system. I might have delirium tremens. Or go insane and hallucinate scenes from someone else's childhood.

Unlike a lot of other chronic dieters, my compulsion is dieting itself. I'm not an emotional eater, per se. I'm an emotional dieter. Restricting food equals self-righteousness. Exercising makes me feel superior, holy, strong of will and limb. On the other ham—I mean, *hand*—cheating brings on the whiplash of shame, guilt, and disgust. Like numbers on the scale, the emotions of dieting go up and down, up and down.

Although I try to make light of it, the humor of chronic dieting wears thin, even if nothing else does. The alternative to riding the emotional highs and lows? Become what my friend Pam described as "one of those happy, self-accepting fat people." That fantasy—of ordering bacon cheeseburgers with a wink and a cheeky "More of me to love!"—lasted approximately five seconds before I vowed never to give up. Although I've quit dozens of individual diets, quitting dieting, as a way of life, would be the ultimate defeat.

My most recent diet was inspired by *The Biggest Loser,* a reality TV show. The concept was creepy and sadistic and therefore irresistible: Put sixteen grossly obese people of all ages and genders on a ranch in the middle of a desert and make them compete to lose weight for money. As the contestants reduced, they talked to a pantry-cam about feeling reborn, getting their lives back, emerging from a long, lipid-induced waking slumber. Their existential displacement rhetoric was sad as hell. Nearly every contestant cried fat tears of woe or joy, and so did the TV audience (at least, I did). I knew I was being manipulated, but didn't care. Watching the contestants' gradual transformations—physical and emotional—over the course of a few months was downright inspiring.

For the competition part of the show, the contestants were weighed on a livestock scale. Some would routinely shed ten, fifteen, twenty pounds *in a single week.* One guy lost nearly fifty pounds in just three weeks. I'd been struggling to lose twenty pounds for fifteen years. Granted, the contestants started out at 400 pounds. By their standards, I was already an "after." Everyone knew the last twenty pounds was always the hardest. Still, I convinced myself that my Medium-Sized Loser diet would be a snap.

D-day arrived, as it always did, on the first Monday after I got my period after the last major holiday. My inner announcer said, "Start your engines," and I was off and running—or, more accurately, jogging. I was *ready*. I was *pumped*.

I was doomed.

However misguided optimism might be, you can't begin a diet without total commitment. Otherwise, it'd be like marrying a man you hope to grow to love someday. The Medium-Sized Loser Diet (aka The One) would be strict but doable. The rules:

1. Avoid white food (rice, bread, potatoes, sugar, flour, chips, crackers, etc.).
2. Eat at least six servings of fruit and veggies a day.
3. Drink a glass of water every two hours.
4. Run for half an hour five days per week.
5. Do two thousand crunches per week.

In the throes of the early infatuation period, I was sure this diet would be a piece of (Splendafied) cake. For the record, I did achieve perfection for a solid two weeks. But then life interceded, and my diet was, shall we say, compromised. There was a bake sale at my daughters' school. I would have just bought the minimal face-saving number of cookies, but Lucy gave me the sad look and said, "We never bake anymore." Muttering, I mixed the batter, repeating the mantra "I will not sample, I will not sample." Needless to say, when confronted with fresh-baked cookies, mantras were useless. I ate seven cookies in the span of five minutes.

I had a new novel out, and a rash of lunch and dinner offers from friends and editors with expense accounts. A very-tightwad, I never refused a free meal, especially at pricey places I wouldn't go to ordinarily. When you sat down at a two-star New York City restaurant that was famous for its porterhouse, you didn't dare order the garden salad. It was an affront, an insult to the chef.

The final nail in my diet coffin was my actor/musician husband's three-week gig in Alaska. When Steve got work, he took it, wherever and whenever the job might be, regardless of whether it fit into my diet plans. Since Steve was our family's laundry-doer and vacuumer, his absence doubled my housework load. On top of that, it coincided with the kids' spring break and a major deadline for me. When dinnertime rolled around (every frigging night), I was too tired and stressed to bake the flounder and steam the broccoli. Pizza came to the emotional rescue.

If the timing had been better or I hadn't been stressed out, maybe I would have regrouped. Honestly, though, the air went out of my tires during the bake sale debacle. The first cheat created a domino effect (or, I should say, Domino's). After that, I was cheating regularly, at shorter intervals and with increasing quantities of food per incident. I'd already eaten one slice of pizza, I thought. Might as well have three. What the hell?

It'd taken me six short weeks to go from "This diet is The One!" to "What the hell?" As the saying goes, when I was good, I was very, very good, but when I was bad, I was *horrid*. General Tso's chicken for dinner rolled into bacon for breakfast. I said to myself, "Bacon is Atkins friendly!" I had s'mores with the kids and said to myself, "French women eat chocolate!" My own lies were unconvincing—*even to me.*

When you can't lie to yourself, that's depressing.

The guilt and shame of my failure added up more quickly than the calories I was inhaling freely. Did I cut myself slack for erring, being human? No way! I spiraled downhill, despairing. The diet that began with enthusiasm *had* transformed me—into a depressed, frustrated, stressed-out basket case. Who was three pounds heavier.

When the sugar dust settled, I reverted to the familiar reflective between-diets rest period. I called a couple of diet experts I'd consulted with over the years, shrinks with university jobs who'd become my confidants. Joan Chrisler held up perfectionism as my diet undoing. "Very little in life is perfect. If you expect it of yourself on a diet, you're riding for a fall." I denied trying to be Polly Perfect. "But you begin a diet on 'the first Monday after you get your period after a major holiday,'" she replied. "That's really about finding the perfect time to start the flawless diet."

Ed Abramson put some nuance on that analysis. "It's the all-or-nothing mind-set," he said. "You slip once, and it's over. You see a diet as black or white. On or off. And once you go 'off,' it's no-holds-barred."

Both Joan and Ed talked a lot about motivation. "Why was it so important to diet?" they asked. "Why did you structure your day around an eating-and-exercise plan?"

They might as well have asked, "Why have you structured your entire adolescent and adult life around some eating-and-exercise plan or another?"

Big question. Up there with "Is there a God?" and "If you

eat a cookie in the forest where no one can see, does it still have calories?"

Why diet, indeed?

I tried to come up with a decent answer for the eternal question. Was I attempting to lose weight for my husband? Early in our relationship, when Steve and I first fell in love, I was fifteen pounds thinner. Logically, a swing of fifteen pounds wasn't too significant. I was the same person, regardless of the pants I fit into. Irrationally? Fifteen pounds was a gulf. The difference between a job interview and a job offer. Between a first date and a second date. Between being honored by the nomination and winning the Oscar. The chubby kid I used to be will always wonder which version of me—skinny or fat—is more deserving of love. I knew I'd put pressure on myself to be a good dieter while Steve was in Alaska. I wanted to please him upon his return with a slimmer silhouette. I had the fantasy of his finally walking in the door after three weeks away, dropping his suitcase on the floor, laying eyes on me, running into my arms, and muttering ridiculous sap into my ear, along the lines of "I love you beyond measure, every moment apart was sheer agony, your beauty is boundless," etc.

If not for Steve's sake, perhaps I was a chronic dieter simply out of habit. Diet was what I did. It was all I knew. In fact, dieting know-how had been hardwired into my brain since preadolescence. Thanks to recent advances in MRI technology, we now understand that the brain takes shape according to the stimuli it receives. This was a good argument for forcing a kid to take piano lessons. If she learned to play young, her brain's nerves and synapses would retain musical affinity forever. I didn't play piano. Or chess. My teenage brain was honed, forged, and wrinkled for dieting. Reducing was my chief adolescent pastime. I made charts. I logged calorie input and output. I kept food journals. I read diet articles in magazines, ripped through weight loss books (memorably *The Complete Scarsdale Medical Diet,* released in 1979, when I was fourteen). Diet tips and tricks were snaked so deeply into my gray matter, there was no surgical or psychological way to extract them.

Another "why me, diet?" reason? The nagging one that Joan and Ed always brought up, the one that rang loud and clear. Dieting was, as Ed said, "a convenient channel for life's dissatisfactions. Rather than deal with things that make you unhappy, you narrow the focus to eating."

I'd certainly had my share of problems, and at every stage of life, I'd dieted my way through a lot of the bumpy times—even some hard times you'd think would be immune to the cold comfort of losing weight. For instance, when I was thirty-five, I became a widow. My first husband, Glenn, died of lung cancer. He was only thirty-four. It was an unspeakable tragedy for our family—our daughters were five and almost two when he died—as well as for our extended families and friends. The shock of his death was the prelude to the stress of widowed motherhood, of guiding my daughters and myself through grief, supporting our needs on my income. It was a Herculean holding together. I'd managed it, survived. And, yes, I lost weight during those horrible two years, which didn't cure Glenn or ensure my daughter's emotional protection but did give me something to think about when all other thoughts were bleak.

Of course, I re-gained the weight I'd lost, that time, and every other time I'd managed to lose. This predictable outcome raised the same question: "Why?" Why should I, or anyone, diet at all, when many experts in the field believe, and have supportable evidence, that dieting makes you fat? My Medium-Sized Loser Diet was a case in point. I'd starved myself at first; my body's deprivation mode kicked in, resulting in a slower metabolic rate. When I started cheating repeatedly, those excess calories rushed into a body that was burning fuel at a crawl, instantly converting pizza into fat bulges. With each diet I'd tried, I was farther from my goal weight.

My goal weight, since college, had been 135 pounds. At five feet six inches, that would give me a body mass index, or BMI, of 21.8, dead center of "normal" range. I wasn't greedy. I wasn't shooting for a teen-model BMI of 17. My aspirations were for single-digit clothing sizes, bony fingers, a hollow around the cheeks. I'd had that, at brief and glorious periods over the years. Surely I could have it again, or so I'd reasoned a million times, right before starting each new (soon-to-be-failed) diet.

Diet experts would also insist that dieting was futile. Depending on which study you read, 50 to 90 percent of an individual's weight was genetically predetermined. Or you could see it this way: As an egg in your mother's ovary, you were already a size twelve. Now, you might be able to diet your way down to an eight, or even a stretch-fabric six. But you'd never be a two, no matter how bad you wanted it. If you were to stop dieting and eat "normally" (have what you crave when hungry, stop when full), your body would automatically assume its preprogrammed shape, its true size, with virtually no struggle or anxiety on your part.

I had no idea what my true size was. I'd been yo-yo dieting (sometimes so-so dieting; always oh-no dieting) for thirty years. My metabolism and eating had always been erratic. My body hadn't had the chance to automatically assume its preprogrammed shape. My parents were both naturally slim. My sister was small, my brother athletically built. My grandparents on both sides were either slender or athletic. And yet I was a chubby kid. An anomaly? Or perhaps, had I not been a prepubescent diet cycler, I might have burned off my baby fat naturally—and, just as naturally, grown into a slim adult. Slimness might have been my destiny, but only if I was able to let it happen.

On the other hand, it might have been my destiny to be a blimp.

Only one way to find out. I would have to give up dieting. Logically, it made sense. If dieting made you fat and was futile, not dieting should make you thin, effortlessly.

I'd been listing all the reasons for "Why I Should Diet" in my head for thirty years. At forty-one, perhaps the time had come to make a new list, headed "Why I Shouldn't Diet."

I fantasized about the change, both emotional and physical, about the freedom in reach. I painted a mental picture of what a diet-free life would look like—me, in a sundress, running braless, barefoot, through a field of wildflowers. The idea became a hunger. Not a fleeting craving, but a deep, visceral yearning that, I realized, had always been rattling the cage inside.

I would need a plan. (I might be able to stop the diet cycle, but I would never be able to give up planning.) What would be the opposite of chronic dieting? Regular dieting was about the physical, eating and exercise. The Not Diet would be mental, emotional, concentrating on interior conversations, bad memories, the wiring of my brain. The goal of chronic dieting was to shed pounds. The goal of the Not Diet was to shed light on my self-destructive habits and patterns.

The Not Diet (aka The Last One) would be strict but doable:

1. *Forget everything I already knew about dieting.* That wouldn't be easy. It'd be like tearing out the seams of a dress and wearing it anyway. Trying to be perfect hadn't worked for me, either, so rule number two was . . .

2. *Screw perfectionism.* My wobbly first baby step toward screwing perfectionism was to sit down and eat a bowl of ice cream . . . Okay. Done. And boy, was that delicious. Much easier than I'd thought! I feel confident that I can succeed at imperfectionism. I should call my mother right away and tell her that I've found something I am really good at. Then again, talking (inside my head, or through the lips) about eating hadn't served me well. Ergo, rule number three:

3. *Shut the hell up.* I'd stop the running mental commentary about food, what I see in the mirror, all the things I'm doing/not doing right, comparing myself to other women. I'd silence my mind regarding weight. That'd be tough. Often I didn't even realize I was tallying calories until half an hour had gone by. I resolved to fill my mind with productive thoughts, like getting to the big

bottom of my bad body image. Which dovetails nicely into the final rule of my plan, the whopper:

4. *Do the emotional heavy lifting.* Dieting thus far had been a physical endeavor—and a chronic failure. Perhaps what had been missing all along was the emotional regime, a systematic approach to body image bone picking. Skeleton sweeping. I latched on to the idea that each extra pound I carried on my frame represented a past hurt, an emotional injury that took the physical form of belly fat. If I could let go of the shame, embarrassment, anger, and insult from the past (forgive, forget, whatever worked), my body would release the weight. Into the wind. Like magic!

As I already mentioned, I'm nothing if not optimistic.

"Diets don't *have* to be forever," I said to my sister, Alison. "I've got to stop, or I'll be dieting until I'm too old to feed myself. Knock wood that I should live so long."

The late summer afternoon was sunny and clear. Maggie, Lucy, and I had escaped the Brooklyn heat to spend the day at Alison's home on the balmy North Shore of Long Island.

"Speaking of diets, are you eating bread today?" asked Alison. "I made sandwiches."

Alison could eat bread. Great baskets of it. Except for one fluky, chunky year in high school, she had always been petite. In childhood photos, her legs look like flamingos', stalk thin with knob knees. At five foot three, Alison was small all over. Her feet were a tiny size six, her fingers short. She wore a size two dress. The only big part of her was her thick, curly black hair that pillowed on her bony, narrow shoulders.

Although I was the little sister (fifteen months younger), I'd always been her physical superior—stronger, faster, healthier, *bigger*. Out of the womb, I was inches longer, pounds heavier. Now, I was larger by three inches, four dress sizes, four shoe sizes, and three bra cups. Alison was a pint; I was a pitcher. When we were toddlers, I was considered the pretty sister, and she was the smart one. Now she was both. And I was . . . I was just glad to be here!

If not large, Alison had largesse. Generous as always, she'd laid out a beautiful spread of sandwiches, quiches, and salads for her visitors from the city. Despite our closeness in age and her diminutive size, Alison treated me like a protective big sister would. During the teen years, she'd thrown herself between Mom in full rant and me crying in the corner countless times. Mom's screechy response to her was always, "There's only one mother in this family, and it's not you!" Alison, a mother now, had two daughters (like me; like our mother, Judy). Our four girls, the cousins, were outside while Alison and I talked in the kitchen.

I took a tuna sandwich off the platter. Including the bread. "I've been toying with an idea. Batting it around like a cat with a hair scrunchie," I said. "What would happen if I were to stop dieting? Besides the earth crashing into the sun."

"You mean give up?" she asked.

"I mean stop walking the walk," I said. "Stop talking the talk, thinking the thoughts. I'll probably need a lobotomy."

She nodded. "There's your answer."

"Get a lobotomy?"

"You'll never stop wanting to be thinner," she said. "Every woman wants to be thinner. It's part of the human female condition."

"Okay, yes. That's a given. But I've been going about that quest—thinking about it—the wrong way. What if I did the opposite of what I've been doing all along? Stopped dieting. Stopped obsessing. Go cold turkey on broiled chicken."

"You'll gain," she warned.

"Or maybe, if I purged my bad habits, the bad body image, and the bad memories, the extra weight would disappear."

"Purge the bad memories?"

I said, "Get to the root of my body image problem, and thereby expunge it."

"So you're going to talk to Mom?" she asked, shuddering. "Give me advance warning so I can be five states away."

I'd never had the big talk with Judy about the emotional damage her fatphobia caused me. We avoided that conversation. It seemed pointless, given how much water was under the bridge. We got along famously now, had since my mid-twenties. We enjoyed each other's company and actually looked forward to seeing each other, which we did often. Both my parents were heroic when Glenn was sick and after he died, for which I would always be grateful. There hadn't been a good reason for Mom and me to rehash our ugly past. Maybe our relationship hadn't been strong enough to handle a major confrontation until now.

"Why do you want to do this?" asked Alison.

"I've spent the first half of my life dieting, vacillating between hating myself, depriving myself, and disappointing myself," I said. "I don't want the second half to be more of the same. Anything else would be an improvement. I think it's possible to let go of the obsession without letting yourself go, in terms of weight."

Alison nodded. She saw the logic. "Not dieting, and getting thin in the process," she said. "It's worth a try."

"I've got nothing to lose," I said. Except the self-loathing—and the excess weight.

2

WELCOME TO HELL

I grew up in Short Hills, New Jersey, an affluent suburb of New York City. I went to Deerfield Elementary School. After sixth-grade graduation, some parents sent their children to private schools like Newark Academy or Pingry. Most residents of the Millburn–Short Hills township sent their kids to the highest-ranking public secondary school in the most densely populated state in the nation—Millburn Junior High. My class had three hundred kids. Three hundred lucky, entitled, gifted little shits.

Unlike the almost exclusively pasty-white Jewish kids at Deerfield, the larger student body at MJHS was a real mix. I was introduced to a wider spectrum of white—ecru, eggshell, bone—kids from Irish, English, and Italian families. Lots of new faces. New boys. I started seventh grade with confidence. Despite my extra pounds, I'd been popular at Deerfield, one of only two girls asked on a date in sixth grade. Even though I'd gained weight over the summer and was rotating a fresh crop of zits on my forehead, I assumed I'd be popular in junior high, too.

Within a week of stepping off the bus, I realized how wrong I was.

My downfall was lightning fast. I "floated word" that I had my eye on a certain boy named T., an irresistible green-eyed, sinewy gentile from another elementary school. He didn't crush on me back, though. On the contrary. My attraction was an affront to him, so much so that it called for a hasty, public refusal. He had another boy start a conversation with me during recess. While I was diverted, T. crouched on all fours behind me. He gave the signal, and the other boy pushed me backward. I flew over T.'s back and onto the dusty playground yard. As I lay there, stunned, T. and his cohort high-fived each other and ran away laughing. I heard later that T. explained himself by saying, "I'd never like Valerie. She's too fat."

The tone was set from that day forward. I was *that* girl. Every seventh-grade class had one. The target of cruel, heartless twelve-year-old boys. The transformation from "pretty and popular" to "outcast and ugly" was so abrupt, it took a while for my change in status to sink in. I thought I still had some residual clout. So, unlike the dozen other kids who were harassed for a variety of physical abnormalities, including but not limited to buck teeth, shortness, and thick glasses, I was not going to take it without fighting back. I might have been chubby, but I was not then, nor would I ever be, a wimp.

Granted, if I'd accepted the abuse quietly, the junior sadists probably would've gotten bored with me and moved on to any number of girls who were far fatter than I was. But I just couldn't keep my mouth shut. "Cocksucker," "dick-breath," "douchebag," "motherfucker" flowed from my twelve-year-old lips like sweet nectar. I learned quickly which buttons to press. Interestingly, nothing got a boy more riled up than being called a "faggot." I flung whatever shockingly offensive slurs popped into my head. Words were my only defense.

Unfortunately, foul language wasn't enough. I was alone against a cabal of hyperactive boys. They egged each other on, ganged up, boosting their status with each other by escalating their vituperation on me. Insulting me became a quick and easy way for any kid to gain favor with the popular boys. The fattest, ugliest, stupidest kid in the class could walk up to me, say "pig," and, for a nanosecond, be "in" with the assholes.

My comebacks started to sound as desperate as they were. About six months into seventh grade, I gave up. I absorbed the blows without retort. But my acquiescence didn't stop the abuse. By now, boys teased me out of habit.

When I'd talked as an adult about my junior high career as a human target for slings and arrows, people always asked, "What about the girls?" Junior high girls were, without a doubt, as a population, the most savage, cannibalistic, cruel subgroup in our nation. However, in my pathetic case, the Mean Girls, the Queen Bees, and the Wannabes left me alone. I wasn't a challenge to their social status. I was hardly competition for cute boys. Certainly, if my name came up in their private conversations, I was assailed or written off. Some girls laughed along when the boys teased me. By and large, however, I was a hapless victim—already wounded—and not a threat. I probably grossed them out, if anything. I barely registered on their radar.

But when *boys* smelled the fresh blood of the emotionally wounded, they became more excited. Thumbnail sketches of my three chief tormenters:

X.'s style was as subtle as a sledgehammer. He'd race up to me and knock the books out of my arms. When I bent down to pick them up, he'd say, "Look at that fat ass." He'd moo and oink. The scariest times were when he'd corner me in the hallway, and hiss *"fat!"* right into my ear. He was in the C track, which was for borderline special ed students. Among all my repeat abusers, X. seemed genuinely unhinged, a powder keg waiting to blow. The rumor mill had him arrested for vandalism as well as breaking and entering. I'd heard gossip his dad beat him up. X. was a notorious beer guzzler, starting in eighth grade. I'd seen him once in the twenty-plus years since graduation, at a mutual friend's wedding. Even though he'd done nothing with his life and looked like a hollow shell of the vicious whelp he used to be, X. terrified me just by standing there.

Y. was a scrawny, lizard-faced rich boy. He seethed with rancor at me and the other targeted kids as if he were personally insulted by our very existence. If he'd been born in another time and place, Y. would have been a crackerjack teenage Nazi. Unattractive, uncoordinated, of average intelligence, Y. had fantastically wealthy parents who gave him everything he wanted, including a BMW when he turned seventeen. Spoiled and rotten, he was just smart enough to be truly hurtful. Y. and I were in the same eighth-grade homeroom. He chose to sit in the desk immediately to my right. My abusers always wanted to be near me, in a twist on the Stockholm syndrome. Anyway, Y. muttered insults across the aisle for the first fifteen minutes of the day, every day. One memorable morning, he said, "When I grow up, I'm going to fuck every beautiful woman I want. I'm going to drive the fastest cars, wear the best clothes. I'm going to live in a big house and have people wait on me. I'm going to be the president of my own company and have millions of dollars. And all you're ever going to be is fat." I was shocked by his delusion. This was an okay student. He didn't play sports or have girlfriends. And yet he knew he'd always be better than me.

Z. was the smartest jackal in the pack. He was also a gifted athlete and a charismatic leader. He was cute, in a suburban New Jersey sense, big hair, big smile, thick gold chains around his neck. His abuse style came close to clever, which, despite my misery, I appreciated. One example: The DJ at a bar mitzvah party started a game of Name That Tune by playing a few notes of "She Loves You" by the Beatles. Z. stood up and said, "That's Valerie's favorite song: 'She Loves Food.'" Humiliating! But sort of funny. Another time, the whole grade was in the school auditorium, watching an educational film. I was seated on the side, with a couple of my friends. Z. and his cronies piled into seats directly behind me (see above, re: sick Stockholm syndrome). I tensed, waited for it. On the screen, a shot of the quarter moon. Z. said loudly, "Look, Valerie took a bite out of the moon." Uproarious laughter, drawing the attention of the entire class, forcing the AV technician to stop the film and a teacher to demand to know what was so flipping funny, etc. Unlike most of my tormentors, Z. was A track, like me. Out of class, he made fun of me. Often, during class, he spoke to me respectfully, even affectionately. I was convinced that, on some level, Z. thought we were friends. Boys trash-talked each other to bond. Z. might've believed that abusing me, which he not only did but encouraged others to do, was a way of saying, "You're one of us." For this reason, I hated him the most of all.

I existed in a state of constant anxiety. The fear was mainly anticipatory, like how people feel about terrorism today. Although each embarrassment was horrible, waiting for the next was worse. The constant guesswork—When would it happen? Where would they strike?—shifted the bedrock of my personality. Since I was perpetually braced for an insult, I felt relieved when it came. It always came.

A couple of teachers joined the fun. Men. The type who were the ass-kissing followers when they were in middle school, the grown-up boys who sought the approval of the X.s, Y.s, and Z.s of the world.

A math teacher, considered creepy and lecherous by all the girls, made a special announcement one day: He'd noticed a lot of negative attention was being paid to one particular girl, and teasing from a boy really meant that he had a secret crush. This comment brought on a tsunami of abuse that lasted for weeks. Any idiot could have easily predicted it. I was sure that math teacher knew exactly what he was doing.

A science teacher, a former wrestler with a menacing posture, made a point of calling on me in class to answer questions about food. For a lesson on the unit measure of heat called a calorie (at fourteen, I already possessed doctoral-level knowledge on the subject), he wanted to know what students had for breakfast. I didn't raise my hand. He called on me anyway. I fumbled for a response that sounded sufficiently Spartan, but not self-consciously so, and eventually stammered out the word "bread." The teacher mocked me. "Bread? What do you mean, *bread*?" It was an open invitation, the granting of permission, which X. and a few other boys in class jumped on as if it had been a drunk cheerleader. "A loaf," said X. "Two loaves." "A dozen bagels," "five cakes," etc. While the boys competed to shout out the most outrageous quantity of carbs I was to have consumed in a single meal, I stared at the science teacher's face. I kept staring, for the remainder of that class, and every other to follow. He was spooked by my unblinking glare of pure hatred, and he never made eye contact with me again.

Unlike a lot of harassed kids who took their lumps at school, I did not, alas, have a supportive, nurturing safe haven at home. School was the frying pan; home was the fire. After enduring the agony of the junior high day, I'd get home and sink into the living room couch. It was exhausting, keeping the game face on for hours upon hours. I just wanted ten minutes to decompress. But then Mom would walk into the room, look at me sprawling, and say, "Go run around the block, for Christ's sake. Don't just sit there. Do *something*. Who gave you permission to have a snack? You can't eat that. The Ring Dings and Twinkies are for your brother. Give it to me now. Give me that Ring Ding!"

I broke down only in private, music blasting in my room to cover up the violent adolescent sob fests, flailing on the bed, pummeling my pillow. In public, I was unshakable. I learned to feign indifference so well, it became instinctual.

To this day, when I receive bad news, my eyes go flat. My face loses any hint of expression—what forehead-to-chin Botox probably looks like. I show nothing. I give nothing away. A boss fires me from the first real job I ever had and won't give me a reference? Okay, I say, see you never. An editor gives me a massive revise memo on a novel I'd worked on for a year? No problem, I shrug, whatever. Even the worst possible news, the moment it was delivered, failed to ripple my exterior. When the oncologist arrived in Glenn's hospital room late one evening and told us what the biopsy had revealed, stage IV lung cancer, I merely nodded, flat-eyed. The doctor repeated himself. Did I hear what he just said? Did I understand what this meant? Was I even paying attention?

For the record, I've heard every syllable of every horrible thing that's been said to me, in junior high and since. My ears prick up to catch the slightest intonations, the smallest hint of negativity, even in a seemingly benign comment. I was, am, a connoisseur of insult and criticism. My word-for-word analysis reveals the deeper meaning of what wasn't said. Down to the pumping core of my heart, when a boy spat, "This hallway isn't big enough for you," I knew he was confessing to me (and only me), "I'm desperately insecure and have to boost my ego by insulting you." I possessed secret knowledge, an intuitive power of observation and understanding that pretty girls lacked. Like alienated teenagers everywhere, I wrote down my revelations and thoughts, since they were important, real, and deep, and had never been thought of by another person before, nor would they ever be in future.

I kept a journal. A blank book with a red corduroy cover. On the pages, I wrote angsty poetry ("Caverns of darkness/ dungeons of punishment/palisades of cruelty/the light of happiness never shines here"), and I wrote stories. My main character was named Sal. She had an evil mother who said, "So what if you got an A on the Spanish quiz? You'll just fail the next one. Jesus H. Christ, Sal, I'm just teasing. Stop that pathetic sniveling." Sal was an adequately pretty girl with a "fat layer that had to go." She was routinely belittled by her overachiever older sister and hostile younger brother, misunderstood by her friends, and mistreated by her parents and everyone else. But—Sal had a secret. When she retreated to her attic room after a wretched day of torment, she lay on her pallet bed of straw and mud and meted out justice. Sal had magic powers. Anything she imagined came true.

Sal was a wee bit bloodthirsty. X., Y., and Z. died a hundred times on the pages of my blank books, each death more grisly and savage than the last. They were eaten alive by dogs (Sal said, "Slow down, puppies, or you'll get tummy aches!"), pulverized by a speeding garbage truck ("Don't bother bagging them," said Sal to the driver), skateboarded into a sinkhole (Sal said, "Did I say turn *right*? I meant *left*. Oops."). Drowning, dismemberment, suffocation. Their female cohorts—girls who laughed along—met similar sorry fates. Complicity was just as bad, by Sal's rule of law. If a girl stood by and watched Z. verbally assault Sal, well, she deserved to die ignominiously, too. Oddly, Sal never used her magical, deadly thoughts against her family. Even for someone with the questionable morals of a killing machine, murdering one's own blood seemed wrong.

I remember cackling wildly to myself when I wrote these stories. It helped to vent. Back in the 1970s, misunderstood and mistreated kids didn't go around shooting their bullies with AK-47s. Nowadays, when I read about another school rampage, about the awkward, unstable kid with a gun, how he just couldn't take one more day of humiliation and how he'd long fantasized about revenge, I deplore it. I'm saddened and sickened by it. But I understand it.

Of course, for every kid who goes ballistic, there are a hundred thousand teens who suffer in depressed silence. Some find ways to mitigate their suffering. I scribbled bloody comedies in a journal and laughed at my own jokes. Lo and behold, I grew up to be a comedy writer who still laughs at her own jokes. Humor is a coping mechanism for dealing with pain.

What doesn't kill you only makes you funnier.

I rehashed this theory to my friend Rebecca at Teresa's, a Ukrainian diner on Montague Street in Brooklyn Heights, where we both live. We were having breakfast. I was not-dieting, but also not-hungry. Talking about junior high made me feel a little queasy.

"You have to eat the rat," she said.

"Excuse me?" Make that a lot queasy.

"You never heard that phrase? It's from G. Gordon Liddy."

"The Nixon stooge?" I asked.

"He had a lifelong fear of rats," said Rebecca. "So one day, he decided that the only way to overcome his fear was to consume it. So he cooked a rat and ate it."

"Gross," I said. "Bet it tasted like chicken."

"Your goal is to get rid of your weight obsession. Part of your obsession is connected to these assholes from junior high," said Rebecca. "You have to track one of them down. Make contact."

"And eat him?" I asked. "Chew him up and spit him out?"

"Just call him," said Rebecca.

"No way," I said, a cold chill instantly creeping up my spine at the very idea of confronting X., Y., or, especially, Z.

"You must," said Rebecca. "And you will."

Over the coming days, the images of their acned teenage faces kept floating into my consciousness. I wondered what they might look like now. Ideally, they were bald, *fat,* divorced, unemployed, friendless, loveless, depressed, suicidal, one-legged, and living with their parents—correction, homeless.

Tentatively, I did some light Googling. This yielded zero useful information. I was relieved. If I had turned something up, I would've had to use it.

For tenth grade, students left the junior high building and went to the high school down the road. The move was a welcome change. In the new building, the evil boys seemed to forget about me. I was still a loser, but I wasn't attacked hourly anymore. I struggled to fit in, to blend, to be just another girl walking the hallways. I befriended other girls like myself. Many of these friendships lasted as long as the diets we'd start together (with enthusiasm!) and then abandon (in defeat).

You could share only so many rice cakes before the friendship itself tasted stale, flavorless, a substitute for something substantial. I also hung out with other A trackers. But due to their (our) big brains, free-floating geekiness, Jewishness, and/or eccentricity, they (we) were ignored by the Sassoon-jeans-wearing, gum-snapping, blue-eye-shadowing, blond girl jocks who ruled the school.

The Official Preppy Handbook came out in 1980, the year I was a sophomore. Lisa Birnbaum's humor book became my survival guide for living in WASP-dominated Short Hills. My mother was relieved I'd taken a sudden interest in my outward appearance, and my closet filled up with Fair Isle sweaters, corduroy skirts, grosgrain belts, handbags with wooden handles and removable canvas pouches. With a panting determination, I flung myself into preppiness (which, I should have known, given my ample chest and frizzy hair) was yet another impossible dream. I signed up for the JV field hockey team, the epitome of preppy sport.

We had practices every day after school. My mother encouraged my participation. If I were running laps around a field, I couldn't be at home, shoving Ring Dings into my piehole. Although most of the girls on the team sat at the popular table and, therefore, had associative revulsion for me, they treated me politely. Their niceness caused me some guilt. A number of these girls had died painfully under Sal's swinging axe. The coach, a megalomaniac, encouraged team bonding. She chose the first-string lineup and team captains— power positions that popular girls lusted for. We did what Coach wanted, and that meant maintaining a perpetual state of "Psyched!" on the field.

I didn't have ambition to be a first stringer, or a captain. I just wanted to be one of them, another rosy-cheeked pretty girl in a kilt with a stick. I was suspicious of Coach, who seemed overly serious and intense about her team. This was New Jersey, not Texas. The Friday night lights in Short Hills were at the mall, not the football stadium. The town's pride and glory did not rest on the shoulders of the girl's JV field hockey team. Nonetheless, Coach acted as if every practice were a matter of life and death. Granted, some of the gifted players would go on to varsity and possible scholarships to college. Or they came from athletic families and felt the pressure of expectation. Not me. I just wanted to be a player.

But players weren't cynical. I'd had cynicism beaten into me during the junior high years. My snide little comments and sarcastic observations weren't considered insightful or witty by the other girls. I was never initiated into the unofficial team sorority. On the bus to games, I watched the girls get "pumped" and "rowdy" while singing "We Are the Champions," smashing their sticks to the beat on the floor, their faces contorted in competitive fury. I though they looked like escapees from a juvenile prison. I didn't get it. It was only a game.

At the time, I thought of Coach as a middle-aged bachelorette gym teacher who ruled her tiny fiefdom with an iron whistle in order to give her lonely life meaning. The years since have softened my opinion of her. She took herself and her job seriously. She showed pride in her work and had more insight than I gave her credit for. For example, Coach could tell I had selfish reasons for being on the team: to fit in, get out of the house, and try another weight loss strategy. I lacked "heart" and "spirit." Once, Coach said to me, "Frankel! There's no 'I' in team." I said, "No, but there is a 'me.' Also 'at,' 'eat,' 'met,' 'meat,' 'tame,' 'mate,' and 'meta.'" Coach was not amused or impressed by my anagram ability. "Ten laps around the field, Frankel," she barked. "Go!"

My father, Howie, a nephrologist, came home one evening during my field hockey season with a few boxes of a prototype protein powder supplement called Optifast. Protein supplements in liquid or powder form are now available at any supermarket, but back then, replacing solid food with protein shakes for rapid weight loss was a radical treatment that required the supervision of a licensed physician. Optifast was not yet available to the general public. I was to be a guinea pig for the product, under my father's care.

Pause to ponder the wisdom of putting an adolescent, only ten pounds overweight, on an experimental medical protocol for aesthetic reasons only.

Okay, we're back.

Not to cut Dad too much slack about the Optifast initiative, but I believe he brought the box home because he was desperate for peace. Although the evil boys had matured enough to leave me alone, my mom was stubbornly one-noted. She beat the weight loss drum constantly. I heard it in my sleep. Whenever I entered the house, she was there, tall and slender, a stalking dark-haired, dark-eyed menace, monitoring my after-school snack. At dinner, she commented on my rapid chewing, request for seconds, daring grab at a dessert. On weekends, the stress of being around me and my fat accumulated for two days. It was too much for her. She'd explode on Sunday nights and scream at me for purposefully antagonizing her by eating. "You're so fat!" she'd shriek. "Why are you doing this to me?" Alison continued to defend me, which led to more fighting and yelling. I'd hide in my room, crying in fits, blasting music to cover the sound. Not traditional Sunday-night family fun. When Dad got wind at the hospital about the promising new product for weight loss, the lightbulb must have burst into flames over his head. He must've thought Optifast would be the answer to all our family's turmoil. So Optimistic. And so wrong.

The unflavored powder, mixed with water, tasted chalky and gritty, nothing like the chocolaty Slim-Fast shakes you can get today. I choked it down each morning for breakfast. My lunch was a banana and a yogurt. Dinner: another shake. For two weeks, I was perfect (hence, doomed), essentially fasting, and working out like a dog at field hockey practice. As advertised, I enjoyed "rapid weight loss." Fifteen pounds in two weeks. According to weight charts for someone my gender and age, I was officially one pound underweight.

My parents acted like they'd discovered religion, praising the Lord, thanking God, declaring a miracle. I can picture my mother on the phone with her friends, crowing about her success. I reveled in the change, too, as I always did when I dropped weight. I strutted around school, cocky and arrogant, my clothes baggy. My few friends were full of compliments. Mom had to adjust my kilt's snaps, since it kept falling down during laps. I was tired on the field, slower, but Coach, along with everyone else, liked what she saw. She seemed more tolerant of me.

High on downsizing, I was smug and, therefore, vulnerable

to attack. One morning, a boy, P., got bawled out by our homeroom teacher for being late to school. I looked over at him, a couple of desks behind me to the right, his face bright red with embarrassment. I knew exactly how he felt, having been singled out back in my heavy days, which were, thanks to Optifast, now gone forever. I shot P. a look of sympathy, which he must have interpreted as gloating. Narrowing his eyes at me, he said, "Fuck you, Frankel. You're fat."

Simple, clean, plain. Unadorned abuse from a kid on the spot, lashing out defensively at a usual target. Three weeks before, I would have considered it my due. But . . . but . . . couldn't he see that I was officially underweight now? I'd lost fifteen pounds. I'd consumed liquid chalk and baby food for two weeks straight. I'd been starved by my own parents, one of them a doctor, and yet this kid P., an A tracker, not blind or stupid, said "fat" as if I hadn't suffered and changed. He, and probably everyone at school, would always see me as fat. I'd have to go full-blown anorexic (like a couple of other formerly overweight girls) to be considered normal by my classmates.

I was devastated. I'd been off Optifast for less than a week. That afternoon, I started making up for lost snack time. I skipped practice three days in a row. When I finally showed up, I smoked in the locker room before and after. I blew smoke rings at the popular girls with cinched waists and blond hair, none of whom were my friends. I bolted as quickly as possible each afternoon, and I missed a team announcement. The homecoming game against our bitter rival was a week hence. On that day, the rookie JV players, in an initiation tradition, were to wear their kilts to school with high heels.

When I showed up in jeans, I was yelled at by the other players, who all looked pretty good in their kilts, heels, and giraffe-thin legs. I called Mom and asked her to drive over my skirt and the earth-toned platform shoes with Naugahyde straps across the arch and ankle. I changed as soon as I could. I'd been eating at will for a week since P.'s comment, and I'd regained most of the weight. The kilt, with its resewn snaps, was now supertight around the waist, making the hem ride up, revealing as much leg as I had. My panties showed when I bent even slightly. My bloomers, alas, were still in my underwear drawer at home, and I didn't dare call Mom again and ask her to bring them down to the school. I put on my platforms, tugged my kilt down, and went on with my day.

As if. Boys followed me through the halls, laughing at my bulging belly and visible underwear. I walked into the cafeteria at midday as slyly as possible and tried to hide in a corner. A friend said, "Everyone is staring at you." I glanced around the room. Table to table, all eyes were on me. I felt faint. My friend walked me out of there and into the nearest girls' bathroom, where I puked up my nerves and lunchroom fried chicken.

I went to the nurse's office, said I was sick. Mom came to get me and, for once, showed mercy by not asking questions or making comments. I found out later that the girls on JV told everyone I was a wimp for leaving, that I couldn't take a joke, that I didn't have team spirit, that they knew I wasn't really sick, that if I puked it was because I was bulimic, that I smoked in the locker room, which made all of them want to puke, on me, and that I sucked as sweeper, because I couldn't run fast enough, because I was fat.

In the movie version, I would have proved them all wrong. I'd have dug in my cleats, doubled up on practice, kept running around the field in the pouring rain when everyone else had already gone home. I'd have saved the big game in the last second and been redeemed, forgiven, accepted, beloved by my teammates and the entire school.

In the reality version, that day marked a turning point for me. It was the day I said "fuck this" about trying to be accepted.

Almost immediately, I was cut from the team. I forced the issue with Coach when I refused to leave school early for an away game. I'd have had to reschedule an exam. I told her that academics were more important than sports, and if she didn't agree, she was wrong and, for that matter, irresponsible in her position as a "teacher," albeit a gym "teacher." I actually used finger quotes. It was the most flagrantly disrespectful and rude thing I'd ever said to an authority figure. I was sixteen. It was an exciting new beginning.

There was bitterness in triumph. In my journal, I wrote, "I was cut from the team today. I felt like crying but I kept it bottled up in school. As soon as I got home, Mom said, 'You're not good at sports anyway. I knew this would happen. How could you expect to keep up with those other girls?' I stared at her for a while, and then ran to my room to cry."

Instead of heeding Mom's suggestion that I try candy-striping, I spent my afternoons scribbling frantically in my blank book. Sal had an extended field day on the field hockey team. And then I shoved every grosgrain belt, Fair Isle sweater, and duck print skirt into the back of my closet, never to be worn again. "Preppy" became synonymous with "assholey" to me, an opinion that has not evolved much. Whenever I see a grown woman in a velvet headband, I automatically distrust her.

Fitting in, being part of a whole, finding my place in the social order, being appreciated by my peers was suddenly, blissfully, irrelevant.

Along with the clothes, I shed any semblance of mainstream ambition. I'd been a stealth smoker since the eighth grade. I would walk a mile to the nearest restaurant and put seventy-five cents into the vending machine for my Marlboro Lights and smoke them on the roof or behind our house. Cigarettes curbed appetite, after all. If I got caught, I would use that as my defense. Except for my provocative puffing in the locker room, I hid my habit because popular kids didn't smoke. Once I'd accepted that I would never be popular, let alone tolerated by our school's Ruling Class, I lit up whenever, wherever I could. High school students were permitted to smoke on the Patio, an outdoor slab of concrete with a few benches by the cafeteria. The Patio and its undesirable residents—the punks and freaks—quickly became my new home and family. Pot came next, great billowing purple clouds of it. Too bad, the munchies counteracted the appetite-suppressing powers of cigarettes. To my bliss, stoners and punks couldn't care less about size. We cared about getting more pot, going to rock shows in the city, driving aimlessly around town, and sharing our intellectual superiority and deep thoughts about meaningful shit, like life, the universe, and the Clash.

I embraced my outcast status. I shaved my hair into a

Mohawk and dyed it orange; I wore safety pins in my ears, spiked dog collars around my neck, black lipstick, black nail polish, black jeans, shirts, trench coats, leggings. I wanted to look as tough as I felt (I had, after all, committed epistolary murder hundreds of times), and so scary that no one would dare mess with me. Punk rock lyrics about isolation, frustration, and alienation described my feelings perfectly. I doubt any of those skinny Brit heroin addicts could possibly have imagined that their lyrics would ring the bell of an upper-middle-class chubby Jewish girl from suburban New Jersey. I seized the message—"Anger can be power, d'ya know that you can use it?" preached Joe Strummer—and made it my mantra, my mien, my modus operandi.

Mom's rants weren't so monotonous once I gave her more notes to play. "That outfit is disgusting!" she'd screech. "You reek of cigarette smoke! I hate your juvenile delinquent friends. You're not doing your schoolwork! Turn off that horrible music! And put down that Twinkie!" Mom did approve of one change. My new black wardrobe was slimming.

Rebellion became my cause. Anything that pissed off my mother and entrenched me as an outcast was my pleasure. My punk friends and I drove to clubs in New York—CBGB's and Great Gildersleeves—to see hardcore shows. We'd stay out until 2:00 A.M., then drive back to New Jersey drunk on Meisterbräu. I'd stumble home, steal into the kitchen, and inhale the contents of the fridge. I shoveled it in, every bite a "fuck you" to my mother. She always heard, too. Over the years, she'd developed a sixth sense that told her whenever I ate anything with calories (aka anything except celery). The crunch of a single potato chip would awaken her in the middle of the night as if it were a dozen air raid sirens. She'd yell from her bedroom upstairs, waking up the neighborhood, "The kitchen is closed!"

Then I'd go to my room, put on my headphones, sink into the sounds of Public Image Ltd. and the Ramones, and write in my journal. Not that old red one. I'd filled it up stories ago, and had retired many others, too. By eleventh grade, my entries had evolved thematically. My later teenage stories were less violent but equally passionate. They starred Sal as the misunderstood heroine, unloved and unwanted, until a handsome ("cute") hero saw beyond the cigarette smoke, black lipstick, spiked collars, and stomach flab. Instead of Sal slaying the dragons, a conquering hero would do it for her. He'd ride up in his Mustang convertible, vanquish her enemies, cherish her unconditionally, and make mad, hot, gooey love to her.

My romantic fantasies gave me hope. My steady diet of "fuck this and/or you" had brought me adventure, friends, fun, terrible sex. But it hadn't brought me love. That would come later.

3

THE MOTHER LOAD

My mom told me a story the other day about her neighbors in Short Hills. The couple had a son and a daughter. The girl, age ten, was overweight.

I'd seen this kid. She didn't look that fat to me—plump, perhaps—but I was generous about other people's extra weight (so *not* generous about my own, goes without saying). Mom went on to tell me that the chubby girl's mother had been advised by their pediatrician not to talk about weight at home and, instead, outsource the job to professionals. They'd signed her up for weekly sessions at nearby St. Barnabas Hospital for nutritional counseling and exercise tips.

"Let me get this straight," I said. "A healthy ten-year-old girl is going to a *hospital,* where people are sick and dying, to learn how to eat and run."

Mom said, "This is what they do with overweight kids these days. My neighbor said, 'Instead of me riding her, now it's their job.' Children aren't receptive to what their parents tell them."

"You realize you're talking to me, right?" I asked. "You must see the relevance."

"Relevance to what?" she asked.

I should have railed at her, explaining just how receptive I'd been to her homespun version of nutritional counseling ("If I let you make your own sandwich, you'd be big as a house!") and exercise plan ("For Christ's sake, go run around the block!"). Instead, I made up an excuse and hung up. Decades have passed since Mom was in her neighbor's shoes. Back when I was a chubster, overweight kids were a blight, a disgrace, an embarrassment. Nowadays, they are emblematic of our self-indulgent instant-gratification on-the-couch culture. Parents of old were enforcers, will-breakers and disciplinarians. Today, parents are their children's secretaries, enablers, and praise delivery systems.

I felt a wave of envy for this little girl. I would have given my teeth for Mom to leave me alone about my weight and send me to counseling instead.

My only institutional weight intervention was when Mom sent me to Weight Watchers when I was fourteen. She carpooled with the mother of another heavy kid, my sister's friend W. The moms would drop us off at the church entrance for the meeting. W. and I would go inside, get weighed, have our progress marked in booklets (a quarter-pound loss week one, a half-pound gain week two, etc.). For the first few weeks of meetings, we stayed to listen as the fat adults with greasy hair and gray clothing talked about the frustration of hitting a plateau and the bitter triumph of resisting their kids' candy bags at Halloween. The Weight Watchers rep would give an inspirational pep talk about losing a hundred pounds, and I found it sad that, years later, her life was *still* defined by how she was once fat. I don't remember who first suggested that we blow off the post-weigh-in part of the meeting. Probably me. By our fourth week, at our first opportunity, W. and I would sneak out the back door, go to the supermarket across the street, buy junk food, and eat it on the church steps until one of our moms showed up an hour later to drive us home. Many candy wrappers were hidden in the church bushes. After a couple of months of this, W. and I had each gained five pounds. I tried to manipulate the scale by sneaking a toe on the floor during my weigh-in, but the monitors caught me every time. They knew all the tricks. Mom demanded to know why I wasn't losing weight on the program. We had a big fight. In my anger and spite, I flung out the truth of how W. and I spent our inspirational evenings. Mom yanked me out of the Watchers, thereby ending my experience in group dieting.

According to a 2006 Stanford University study, there is a direct link between parental weight criticism and bad body image. Of the study's 455 adult female subjects, 80 percent of those with body-related anxieties (including eating disorders, chronic dieting, and/or appearance preoccupation) reported being teased or criticized by their parents about their weight during adolescence. The study's conclusion: Teenage girls are acutely sensitive about their weight, and a parent's negative comments exacerbate that sensitivity *permanently*. Sure, some criticized girls will grow up to have good body image (whoever they are, I'd like to buy them a Diet Coke), but they are rare exceptions. For the majority of kids with fatphobic parents (roughly one in three, says the American

Obesity Association), an adolescence of enforced diets, weight charting, and harassment will mess them up but good forever. When I read the article about this study in the newspaper, I e-mailed it to Mom. She said, "I saw the article, too. I knew you'd make a big deal about it."

Judy believes that whatever she dished out to me was a trifle compared to what Fay, her alcoholic, manic-depressive, narcissistic mother, did to her. And she is right. I cringe from the stories. When Judy was in ninth grade, she would come home from school and find Fay drinking and smoking in the sunroom of their South Orange, New Jersey, home. Mom was then ordered to sit down and listen to Fay list everything that was wrong with her—hair, weight, height, clothes, manner, the way she sat, the way she spoke, what she said— until Fay was too hammered to continue. At that point, Mom was responsible for undressing her drunk mother, cleaning her up, and putting her to bed.

Judy told me, "She just didn't like me. She told me many times that she started drinking when she was pregnant with me because she was depressed about having another baby." The first child, a son, my uncle, had the responsibility of upholding the family name. In the 1940s, in the Jewish suburban subculture, the boy child was expected to go to college, be a success, make something of his life. A girl child? She was supposed to look pretty and marry well.

Going by what I've seen in old, weathered photos, Judy was a solemn, lovely, delicate child, but she wasn't up to Fay's impossible standards. Petite and feminine, Fay was a legendary beauty on her patch, the Jews-only Mountain Ridge Country Club in West Caldwell, New Jersey. Milton, her husband, was considered an exceptionally handsome, virile, athletic man. As a couple, Fay and Milton were envied and popular. They had full social lives and left their two kids at home under the care of live-in housekeepers.

"Fay was a seductive person," said Judy. "She flaunted her attractiveness and flirted outrageously with other men. I was always embarrassed by that, how she dressed and what she discussed. We'd drive home from the club, me and my brother in the backseat, Fay and Milton in the front, and she'd tell a long story about how some man at dinner propositioned her and asked her to visit him in his apartment in New York. My father liked it. He encouraged her. He took pride in other men's interest in her."

Indeed, Fay and Milton's relationship was overtly sexual. For wedding and anniversary gifts, Milton would routinely give his wife flimsy unmentionables from the local lingerie store. Being a busy dentist, though, he didn't have time to pick out the garments himself. "He gave me money and sent me down to the boutique," said Judy. "Two or three times a year, I had to pick out sexy underwear for my father to give to my mother, starting when I was ten. My mother knew Milton sent me on his gift errands. One year, she was so enraged about it, she threw the box at me."

Fay was jealous of any female who came within five feet of Milton, including Judy. "I was in my midteens when she showed me a photo of Milton I hadn't seen before. He was by the pool, wearing a very tight bathing suit. Fay said, 'I bet this is a real turn-on for you, isn't it?'"

"She was threatened by your relationship with your father?" I asked, sickened and embarrassed on Mom's behalf.

"I suppose," said Judy. "At the time, I counted it as just one more bizarre way for her to humiliate me."

I started to get a disturbing picture of what my mom's childhood in that crazy house must have been like. Fay and Milton behaved like the stars of their own psychosexual soap opera. My mom was their prop girl, criticized when something went awry and ignored otherwise. At the same time, although Fay treated her like an invisible girl, she was relentless about Judy's physical appearance. Even if Mom herself was insignificant, her looks still mattered—as a reflection of Fay. A tall, plump child was out of the question. Fay—the social butterfly, the petite beauty, the fashionable flirt—couldn't stand my mother's height, her dark features, her awkward manner. Mom spent much of her childhood in a protective crouch. I feel for her; I know what it must have been like.

Mom repeated Fay's hypercritical parenting style, to a degree. Fay attacked Judy about everything, including all aspects of her appearance. Judy focused her harassment specifically on my weight. In this regard, Judy showed supreme restraint. She did criticize my hair, posture, clothes, manners, walk, talk, etc., too, but rarely. By my grandmother's standards, Judy let me off easy. In a way, I'm grateful.

During the height of my teen years, when my belly bulge was 24/7 on Mom's mind, she restricted our family's exposure to Fay and Milton. Even before then, we hardly spent time with them. The memories I have of my maternal grandparents are few, but vivid. They took Alison and me to see Carol Channing in *Hello, Dolly!* on Broadway. While walking to the theater, Milton stopped us on the street to show us the bowie knife he had strapped to his forearm under his sleeve. He told us that if anyone tried to mug us, he was ready. The gesture was meant to calm us, but it was terrifying. I never felt comfortable with him after that. As for Fay, I could recount the many disastrous Thanksgivings when she'd start okay and then, after the second drink, mutate into Cruella de Vil before our eyes and lay into everyone and everything until she stormed out of our house in a wild rage to cry in her car, her forehead pressed against the steering wheel.

The classic story was when Fay showed up at our house unexpectedly to take Alison, Jon, and me to a restaurant for lunch. My brother ordered a BLT. The waitress brought the sandwich. My brother, who was five, said he didn't like mayo and refused to eat it. Fay insisted he did like it, that everyone loved mayo. Jon held out for unsullied bread. Fay proceeded to throw a shit fit to rival the most tempestuous two-year-old, screaming at Jon, calling all three of us ungrateful brats, accusing us of hating her, being stooges for our mother. It was shocking to me that an adult could behave that way, be publicly, wildly out of control. All the while, she was puffing like mad on her Vantage cigarettes, the ice clinking in her tumbler of Scotch.

Judy does not drink. She has never smoked a cigarette in her life. My first cigarette was pinched from Fay. She used to keep them stacked in a gold case on her den table. Stealing a handful of smokes was the only plus of going to her house. I'd put them in the pocket of my windbreaker, walk in the woods behind the house, and smoke the ones that hadn't broken.

If Fay barely tolerated Judy when she was under her control, she completely lost her crackers when Judy fled. My parents married very young. Howie was twenty-three; Judy was barely twenty. "Fay hit on all my boyfriends, including Howie," said Judy. "He refused to flirt back. When we got married, Fay decided that he was beneath me and that she hated him. She called me a slut when I got pregnant the first time. When Howie was in the air force, we moved to Texas. Fay and Milton showed up at our house uninvited. I was pregnant with Jon; you and Alison were toddlers. Fay walked in the door and started in immediately. 'Look at your hair, look at your dress. The roast is overcooked, the house is a dump.' We got in a big fight, and my parents turned around and left, flew back to New Jersey. They'd been in Texas less than an hour.

"Fay called the next day," Judy continued. "She said, 'You're a fuck, a shit. You're a whore for getting pregnant three times in four years. You're a slut.' Not that it's ever appropriate to call your daughter a whore, but this was in 1966. It was off the charts. I had a friend of Howie's, a psychologist at the air force base, come over and listen in to my next phone conversation with Fay. When it was over, I asked him, 'So, what can I do about her?' He said, 'Don't speak to her again. Ever.'"

For the record, although she has called me fat and lazy, Judy has never called me a whore or a slut, though I might've deserved such a description circa 1990 in a postmodern, owning-it, sex-positive way. Judy described my punk outfits as "trashy." Mom has called me a bitch often. She's told me to fuck off and described me and/or my behavior as shit. I've called Judy a bitch too many times to count. I've advised her to fuck or screw herself, characterized her as a pile of and/or full of shit, and once, after she'd screamed at me for something totally unfair (can't remember what), called her a cunt. I was seventeen at the time and had been lying on my bed in the dark listening to the Sex Pistols on headphones for, like, thirty hours straight (maybe that was what the fight was about). The English really throw the c-word around. It's like a casual term of endearment to them. No different than an American saying, "Hey, lady."

Judy said, "I don't remember you using the c-word."

"I didn't scream it. It was sotto voce. Even when you were tormenting me and I had to resort to calling you a cunt, I did it with hushed reverence."

"Bullshit!" said Judy, laughing. "You bitch."

"Howie heard me say it," I added. "He looked like he wanted to slap me."

"What would you do," asked Judy, "if Maggie or Lucy glared at you and said, 'You cunt'?"

"I'd say, 'Yes, I can!'"

Despite (because of?) our history, Mom and I are quite close. We're bonded like war buddies. Whenever I have news, good or bad, my instinct is to always call her first. Only Mom can soothe some hurts and say the one thing that'll restore my confidence. I don't sugarcoat my life with Judy; our relationship has never had a rosy paint job. As tirelessly as she dogged me about my weight, she has been an exceptional grandmother. She's been an ardent fan of my novels, bragging to her friends, applauding my efforts, laughing at all the right places, going into bookstores and demanding that they stock multiple copies, sneaking in later to turn them face front on the shelves. During Glenn's illness and after his death, both of my parents excelled, above and beyond, in their emotional support and practical assistance, putting their lives on hold for a year to help in any way. They took Glenn to chemo and physical therapy. Mom babysat, driving to our apartment at a moment's notice. They took turns sleeping over after Glenn died and I wasn't strong enough to be alone. I wonder how the kids and I would have survived those bleak months without them.

Now that I'm a parent, I deeply appreciate all the little things parents do that are overlooked and unappreciated. The lunches Mom packed, the carpooling and schlepping, the birthday parties. She never missed a single recital or match—or, in later years, book reading or public appearance. For the last ten years, Mom has taken her beloved golden retrievers to hospices, pediatric wards, detention centers, and geriatric homes to let the sick, despondent, and old enjoy the warmth and companionship of friendly animals. For such work—it's called pet-assisted therapy—Mom has won awards, including one from the New Jersey Veterinary Association when she brought some joy into the depleted hearts of dozens of New Jersey families who lost loved ones on 9/11. Fearless, Judy ventures into some pretty dicey neighborhoods in Newark to provide four-legged furry affection for those in need.

And yet, for all the love, respect, and appreciation I feel for her now, the fact remains: When I was at a tender, formative, vulnerable age, she was ghastly.

"When *I* was a teenager," she said, "no one expected anything from me. I was a throwaway. A nonentity. I expected a lot from you and Alison. I wanted you to expect great things of yourself."

"What if I'd gotten bad grades?" I asked. "Would you have shifted your focus away from weight and railed about my grades instead?" I asked.

She said, "No, I would have gotten on you about the grades, too."

Judy *was* a martinet about grades, though. Both my sister and brother were class valedictorians, Merit Scholars, Presidential Scholars, award-winning grade-getters. I hovered near the top of my class, but definitely not the tippy-top. I had a reputation, after all. Punks were not geeks. Black leather and straight A's did not go together. I was definitely the only kid in AP biology with a Mohawk. I agreed with my parents that grades were important, learning was essential, the mind was a terrible thing to waste. I worked hard enough. My marks and scores were good enough. God knows, it was a hell of a lot easier to get an acceptable GPA than to lose twenty pounds. My parents' academic pressure was a pain in the ass at the time, but it didn't leave a lasting residue on my psyche. And why would it? My high school class rank and test scores became irrelevant the second I got accepted to Dartmouth. My weight, however, has remained relevant. Plenty of emotional residue there.

If Judy had been born in 1971 instead of 1941, she would have logged a dozen years of therapy before considering marriage and children. Instead, she raced to escape her parents by marrying my dad when she was ridiculously young, finishing college but forgoing a career, popping out kids she would live through vicariously. I sympathize with what she went through. Three kids under four at age twenty-five? It's a miracle she didn't put her head in an oven. Her childhood was stolen by her mother. Marriage and children swallowed her young adulthood. My hardworking dad was largely absent. Mom must have been lonely. As a mother, she was obviously frustrated with me. Maybe if she'd been a drinker, she wouldn't have been so laser-focused on my weight. My friends' parents smoked and swilled like good suburbanites.

Part of me feels ambivalent about blaming Mom for anything that's wrong with my psyche now. She never hit me or chained me to the radiator. She did try to starve me, but only of junk food. Considering the devastating parental abuse so many kids face and have to process as they grow up, I had an easy ride. And if the parenting proof is in the pudding, the truth is, I turned out okay. I'm not an emotional cripple. I have a family, a career, pets, a life. I'm stable and happy.

But. The obligation of a parent—*my* obligation as a parent—is to provide unconditional love as well as discipline and structure. Judy, not a huggy, affectionate person, must've felt unconditional love for her kids, but she sure didn't show it. To my teenage eyes, her love seemed conditional upon my losing weight. She installed body anxiety into my hard drive (*permanently,* you bitch!). She was relentless and degrading to her most sensitive, insecure child. At forty-one, I had a few questions for her about that. And I'd get to them, when the moment was ripe (and I had the nerve).

4

THE FORTY-POUND MARRIAGE

Although I'd been stacked since ninth grade, I'd never been comfortable with my big boobs. They were familiar, *in titu,* reliably there where I left them. They floated in the bathtub, and that could be mildly entertaining. I could smuggle pencils underneath them. They also won the attention of a certain kind of man—not necessarily a good thing.

Women who envy large breasts are not hip to their major drawback: Big tits make you look fat. There are exceptions. Skeletal porn stars with whopper implants look like aliens from Planet Hooter. Dolly Parton long ago achieved the rare and freakish tits-on-a-stick silhouette. By and extra-large, though, women with plus-size breasts project volume. Bird-watchers identify species by gauging the "general impression of shape." Should they catch a fleeting glimpse of a large, flying rectangle with pointy triangle ears, they think "owl." Should girl-watchers catch a fleeting glimpse of a curvy, rounded female with a lot of junk in the front, they think "fat."

I met my first husband, Glenn, at a party I threw to celebrate the release of my first novel. A mutual friend brought him along. We were introduced, shook hands, and then I moved on, performing my hostess duties. The party was a blast, a huge success, talked about by many factions for weeks. But it was a disappointment for me in a crucial regard. Despite my inviting half a dozen ex-boyfriends and a handful of guys I had crushes on, I went home alone.

The next day, I sang the single girl's lament to my friends, one bitter phone call at a time. I was lonely and depressed, I said. There was no one for me. One friend disagreed. He said, "I've got a guy for you." I vaguely remembered meeting this Glenn that he'd invited to my party.

"He liked me?" I asked softly.

He said, "When I asked him what he thought of you, he said, 'I got the impression she's chubby.' And I told him, 'She's not chubby! She's busty!' And Glenn said, 'In that case, hook me up.'"

I wasn't charmed by this anecdote. It took me back to junior high. Still, I agreed to take Glenn's call. We set up a meeting at a club. He showed up with five friends. I brought two and stayed for half an hour. It was long enough to show him that in the hourglass that was my figure, most of the sand was on top. I was chubby in only the right places. He must have been satisfied by what he saw. We started going out.

Glenn didn't know it, but he stumbled into my life during a brief and shining slender period. I was twenty-six and wore a size six dress. My jeans had a 28-inch waist. Glenn was twenty-four. He had the classic male Y-shape: broad shoulders, muscular arms, narrow hips, and long legs. I didn't know that I'd stumbled into *his* life during his one and only buff period. So we met when we both looked our best. Appearance was all that mattered to guys in their midtwenties. To me, too. If Glenn hadn't been working out, if I hadn't been skinny, maybe we wouldn't have started dating, and our lives would have gone in completely different directions.

But we did start dating. Our courtship was a blur of bars, bands, and blowjobs. Glenn was the drummer in a rock band (by night—by day, he worked at a publicity firm). I was his number-one groupie and burned many calories having sex in bathrooms all over the Lower East Side. I chain-smoked, annihilating appetite. In the first flush of infatuation, I wasn't hungry anyway. New Relationship Diet #14 was working wonders. Without any strain, my weight dropped during our first year together. I ran five miles a day and spent a goodly portion of my biweekly paycheck at salons. I wish I had more photos from this era. Despite the fact that I'd never looked better, I was still anxious about cameras and stuck with a lifelong tradition of avoiding them.

Glenn and I got serious. We'd come to rely on each other the way couples do for support, company, sex, fun, friendship. I trusted him, I believed in him. And vice versa. When I looked at myself, I cringed at my flaws. When I looked into Glenn's eyes, I basked in his pure unconditional love. After we got engaged, I wrote a short story for a mystery anthology about a woman whose fiancé left her because she gained fifty pounds. Glenn assured me that he would never leave me, no matter what I weighed. When we signed the ketubah, a Jewish marriage license, before our wedding ceremony, we were told by the rabbi to stand facing each other, holding hands. "Look at each other," said the rabbi. "Is this the person you want to spend the rest of your life with? The person you want to grow old with? The person you vow to love from this day forward?" We said yes, yes, yes. It was one of the few times I saw Glenn cry.

I submitted to being photographed at the wedding. I looked decent. I wore my sister's wedding gown. It had to be let out for me, of course, but it fit well. Glenn fit me well. We meshed. The engagement and honeymoon years were bursting with the activity of starting a life together. Glenn switched jobs and worked hard to prove himself. I was editing articles at *Mademoiselle* magazine by day, writing mystery novels at night. We played house in our Brooklyn Heights apartment (only a few blocks from where I live now). I relished my new role as wifey, cooking elaborate meals for Glenn and our frequent dinner guests. On request, I baked the secret-recipe chocolate chip cookies he craved. For a Valentine's Day gift, Glenn encouraged my culinary talents, giving me two hundred dollars' worth of cookware from Williams-Sonoma. I wasn't particularly motivated to lace up the sneaks and go running, not with a loving hungry husband waiting for dinner in our cozy apartment. I served him on our wedding registry stoneware.

Blessed with a fast metabolism, six-foot-tall Glenn could eat anything and remain slim. When we went shopping together at Key Foods, he threw Doritos and packaged cupcakes into the cart casually, guiltlessly. He'd never dieted a day in his life. If anything, he'd struggled to *gain* weight. That was his rationale for buying junk: If he didn't eat it, he'd get too skinny. If I removed some junk food product and put it back on the shelf, Glenn would toss it back in the cart and say, "If you don't like it, don't eat it." Spoken like a true clueless rube. Naturally, I ate more than he did from those boxes and bags with the crinkly wrapping. Embarrassed by my lack of willpower, I'd sneak a cookie here, a handful of chips there. Presto, the bag would be empty, and I'd have to replace it on the sly before Glenn realized he'd married a hypocrite.

It became a family tradition to go to a nearby sprawling Greek diner for brunch on weekend mornings. Glenn would order fried eggs with bacon, extracrisp home fries, lots of butter on toast. He'd eat all of it, then order pie for dessert. I watched in mock horror and genuine envy. He didn't realize how blessed he was, eating at will.

We'd had opposite childhoods. His mother used to cry and beg and yell at him to eat *more*. He told me stories about secreting food into the napkin on his lap to dump in the trash later, or feeding the dog under the table. His mom tempted him with Hostess snack cakes, literally waving them under his nose. I gave Glenn a detailed account of Judy's fat-phobia, how she'd cried, begged, screamed at me to eat *less*. We'd both had bumpy adolescences, bodywise. Me for being fat, Glenn for being pencil thin. We shared our sad and funny tales while we ate those greasy diner brunches. There were a lot of stories, and brunches to match.

Many married couples adopt each other's habits—good and bad. Glenn got me to quit smoking—good. He stopped pumping iron, and I stopped running—bad. I adopted his casual consumption of junk food. With no cigarettes or exercise to keep my weight in control, I gained quickly. Glenn didn't notice that my shirt buttons were straining, my skinny jeans on the shelf, my girth hidden under sweaters. Or maybe he did notice but chose not to mention it.

Within two years of the wedding, I was up fifteen pounds. I rationalized that I didn't have time to diet. My previous diets were elaborately planned and charted. They ate up hours of my time. I didn't have that kind of leisure anymore—the full-time job editing, my part-time job writing novels, being a well-seasoned wifey.

Glenn was in professional disarray. He'd left his publicity job to work at an indie record label, only to leave there for a position at a music wholesaler. At that company, he jumped from department to department. Finally, he resolved to get an MBA at night. That meant Kaplan classes, applications, testing. He spent a lot of nights away from home. I cooked less often, so we ordered Chinese, Mexican, pizza. Neither one of us had seen the inside of a gym for years. We moved to a different apartment, then moved again a year later.

We always made time for love. At thirty—we'd been married for two and a half years—I got pregnant with Maggie. In my second month, we had a scare. It turned out to be nothing. My doctor assured me the baby was fine. Even so, I decided to stay in bed as much as possible, just to be on the safe side. I ate according to the advice books, meeting my daily requirements for protein, fat, and carbohydrates. To make the baby sweet, as I frequently espoused, I ate plenty of sugar, too. I topped 200 pounds by my ninth month, a gain of sixty. One of my most comfortable pieces of maternity clothing was a pink dress with black buttons. A coworker told me I looked like a watermelon.

I dieted after Maggie was born. *The Zone* by Barry Sears had just come out, and everyone at *Mademoiselle* went on the high-protein diet plan. I lost weight, but not enough. The net gain of the Maggie pregnancy was twenty pounds. Predictably, it was impossible to stay in the Zone long term. With a new baby, a full-time job, a husband in grad school, and book deadlines, I ordered in dinner every night. I chose food I could eat while holding the baby. Pizza, dumplings, falafel. Glenn's classes were at night. The lonely hours were passed feeding Maggie every few hours and feeding myself almost constantly. I got pregnant with Lucy when Maggie was two. I tried harder in that pregnancy to be careful with food. I swam laps, avoided sweets. Nonetheless, the net gain of that pregnancy was another five pounds. For those not keeping score, that was a grand total, thus far, of forty pounds.

The night Glenn and I met, I wore a size six backless minidress. Seven years later, at Lucy's first birthday party, I wore size fourteen stretch jeans.

Forty pounds and four sizes in seven years. If I heard this tale of woe (and "whoa!") about another woman, I'd assume something was horribly wrong with the marriage. No woman would be that self-destructive if she were happy. Overeating was really a cry for help. It was a slow, polysaturated suicide attempt. On the other hand, perhaps a massive swelling was the sign of deep contentedness in a secure marriage. As the old saying goes, fat = happy. Or perhaps my girth increase had nothing to do with the marriage itself. I was just overworked and overwhelmed, so I overate.

Being in the thick of life (as it were), I had little time for introspection. I was too harried to analyze what was happening to my body while it was happening. Perhaps I could turn an analytical eye to that period of my life now. It had been six years since the marriage ended. My kids were older, and therefore easier to parent. I wasn't working at an office anymore. I had time to think and the will to do it. Considering the way our marriage ended (which I'll get to in a minute), critical thinking about it was emotionally impossible for years afterward. Our wedded union was preserved in the amber of memory as special and beautiful and tragic. Until recently, the very suggestion that the marriage was less than ideal would have been blasphemous.

But our marriage—like all marriages—wasn't perfect. Glenn and I were happy more often than we weren't. We argued plenty, usually about negative forces outside our relationship (jobs, families, friends). We were in sync about money, travel, long- and short-term goals, how to raise the kids. I was taxed by Glenn's peripatetic career and by his frequent "What am I doing with my life?" complaints. I wished he'd do more around the house and with the kids. He was irked by my bluntness and impatience. We had children before any of our friends, and we were jealous of their freedom. We envied our single friends and loved hearing details about their sex lives. The night two friends called from their Caribbean vacation to tell us they'd gotten engaged, I cried for an hour, mourning that the thrill of new love was behind me forever. Glenn chafed at the isolation of young parenthood, quietly accepting the predictability of sex with the same person for nine years (although we did a good job of keeping that interesting, even at the very end). Our love and friendship were also predictable, but that was a comfort.

As a couple, we were content. As an individual, I was tired of feeling fat. Years went by of being heavier than I ever thought I'd be. Goal weight was a distant memory and far in the future. Although I thought about my size constantly, I did little to change it. Glenn was supportive when I entered the Zone every several months. He refrained from teasing me when I inevitably failed and started what-the-helling.

In fact, in seven years of marriage, Glenn commented on my weight exactly twice: (1) On a random night, while watching me get undressed, he said, "When you gain weight, it shows in your legs." Besides being hurtful and insulting— and making me feel a blast of pure hate, as I had whenever X., Y., and Z. harrassed me in junior high—Glenn's comment was completely untrue. My flab always went straight to my belly, I informed him, and thereby ended that conversation. (2) At the end of my pregnancy with Maggie, I ordered a basket of sweet rolls with breakfast, and he said, "Take it easy, Val." This one was doubly offensive. Like his previous barb, this one hurt my feelings and made me furious he'd insulted me. *But*—this time, he'd also ruined the "guilt-free" pleasure of eating while pregnant. Incensed, I stormed out of the restaurant, crying, demanding to know how *dare* he tell his pregnant wife what to eat. I was hormonal, gigantic, sweating and cursing. People on the street stared. He was embarrassed, more for me than himself. And that was the last I heard from him about my weight. Ever.

Glenn was conflict-averse, what my friend Nancy describes as "a classic Libra. Nonconfrontational, a people-pleaser." The person in a family or office or peer group who calmed and mollified, Glenn was soothing. He aimed to befriend everyone he met, and succeeded. His appeasing nature worked well in our marriage—to a point. Although his temper flared occasionally (never in public), Glenn was reluctant to be aggressive at his various jobs. He wouldn't, or couldn't. And he wouldn't, probably couldn't, have confronted me about my weight.

I'd made it abundantly clear that my family background was a bit explosive. My mother's love seemed to be conditional upon my size. In this way, she was a bad role model for my future relationships. She'd drummed it into my head that her relentless criticism was because she "wanted the best for me," that she was "doing it for my own good." In effect, her relentlessness was proof of her devotion. That was how she saw it, anyway. She wouldn't let me destroy my own life by overeating. Not while she drew breath.

As to how this related to my first marriage, I have two theories. Theory #1: I gained weight as a test of Glenn's love. A fatty challenge. He insisted he would love me unconditionally. But no one else had. Why should I believe him? Would he still want me if I gained ten pounds? How about twenty? Thirty? Forty? Perhaps I would have continued to gain to challenge his commitment until I exploded like the fat man in Monty Python's *The Meaning of Life*.

I've often wondered just how heavy I'd be today if Glenn and I were still married.

Then there's Theory #2: Gaining wasn't a test; it was a

relief. In our marriage, for the first time in my life, I had room to breathe, to eat what I wanted, to be as lazy as a cat in the sun, without fear of scrutiny or abuse. I believed he loved me, would never leave me. I relied on Glenn's distaste for conflict. I took advantage of his benevolence and indulged myself heartily, wantonly, selfishly.

Both theories could be true. I pray Glenn was also too busy and overwhelmed by life to analyze our marriage. I hate the idea that he knew, even subconsciously, that my explosive growth was an attempt to either test him or take advantage of him. It was probably a little of both. For that, I am deeply sorry.

The new millennium arrived with resolutions. On New Year's Eve 1999, I vowed to get serious about dieting. No more of my usual on-for-two-weeks, off-for-two-months diet cycling. Maggie, four, and Lucy, one, deserved a healthy mother they could be proud of. Glenn deserved to get in bed each night with the slender bride he married, not the behemoth I'd become. Turning thirty-five that year, I was still young enough to get back in shape. It wasn't too late for me to improve myself.

But it was too late—for Glenn. In the winter, he'd switched jobs yet again. He thought the stress was responsible for his increasingly severe back pain. In the spring, he saw a doctor about it and went through a series of X-rays and MRIs. He checked into a hospital for more tests to confirm the worst. The back pain was caused by a malignant metastasis on his spine. He also had multiple brain lesions, too many to count. The diagnosis was lung cancer, stage IV. Glenn was a nonsmoker; his doctors called the cancer a fluke, not his fault, which provided zero comfort. In the summer, he had surgery, radiation, and chemo. Nothing worked. He died in the fall, November 3, 2000. He was thirty-four.

In the five months between diagnosis and death, Glenn relived his childhood struggle to gain weight. He dwindled to skeletal proportions. Watching the ravages of his disease was soul- and appetite-killing for me. I lost interest in food. I dropped twenty-five pounds, and two dress sizes, seemingly overnight, effortlessly.

And I was thrilled about it.

Yes, my husband was dying. I was on the verge of widowhood at thirty-five. My daughters were losing their father. I was lonely, frustrated, heartbroken, horrified by the toll illness took on Glenn and everyone else who had a front row seat. Still, despite the sorrow, I took supreme joy in my increasingly roomy clothing. With giddiness in my heart, I'd reach for the thin clothes in my closet. I'd worn a pair of red jeans on our honeymoon and hadn't been able to squeeze myself into them for years. A few weeks postdiagnosis, I was able to get them over my hips. A month later, I could zip them halfway. Another month, I could zip them—and breathe. Another few weeks, they were loose. I smiled dreamily as I beheld my shrinking self in the mirror. Glenn had half a dozen painkillers and antidepressants to ease his suffering. Weight loss became my Vicodin, my Prozac. The red jeans were my delivery system. It took the edge off my pain. Shrinking calmed me, pleased me, gave me something to feel good about.

I shared my secret joy with no one. Who would understand that I could find any reason to be cheerful, given the
grim reality of disease that loomed over us and defined our
days? There was ordinary life, schlepping the kids to school
and playdates, working, shopping, cleaning. Then there was
cancer life, the blur of appointments, driving to hospitals and
doctors' offices for chemo and transfusions, reading about
treatments and therapies, organizing visits so Glenn wasn't
exhausted by too many people at once, dealing with insur-
ance companies, explaining haltingly to Maggie why Glenn
had lost his hair, his energy, his appetite, apparently his interest in her. Lucy was still in diapers, a baby, not yet talking.
Cared for by our beloved babysitter, Lucy was more or less
ignored by me during those five months. I'm sure that'll
come back to haunt me.

Most of all, I spent hours in bed with Glenn, talking to
him, watching TV and movies with him, feeding him when
he could eat, helping him stretch his weakened muscles, reassuring him that he'd beat the disease after every test revealed
that the tumors were growing, had spread. We tried guided
visualization together, lying flat, imagining a magic blue light
had entered his body to wash away the cancer. He went along
because it relaxed him. Rationally, he thought the practice
was stupid; tumors wouldn't shrink just because you willed
them to. Glenn had often said that willpower alone wouldn't
be enough at a job or at school to achieve success. Willpower alone had failed me on diets a hundred times. But we
held on to hope. Which, in this crisis, was another word for
denial.

The glittering blue magic light didn't shrink Glenn's

tumors. But he shrank, as did I, almost at the same pace. Cancer Diet #1 was a success, almost *against* my will. For once, I lost weight without trying. I had conscious thoughts about it, along the lines of "Be careful what you wish for" and "So *this* is what bittersweet tastes like."

I had conscious thoughts, also, that the weight loss would help me when I started dating again. At first I could imagine a life without Glenn only theoretically. But as his cancer spread, my self-preservation instinct set in. I would live, after all, even if Glenn didn't. I was thirty-five years old. A loveless, celibate rest-of-my-life was unthinkable. Instead, I imagined the highly thinkable: that one day a man would come into my life, sex me up, fall in love, marry me, and be a stepfather to the girls. This rosy vision helped me get through some grim moments as Glenn got worse. Losing weight, in part, made my survivalist daydreams possible—or I should say *credible*. It was true when I was single a decade ago, and it would be true a decade from now: Men prefer to date slender women. My slimmer silouette would be a huge plus, whenever I was ready to take advantage of it. Glenn and I never discussed whether he wanted me to marry again or to be his widowed bride for eternity. I was sure he'd expect me to at least try to be happy. I wondered at the time if my subconscious was hard at work during Glenn's illness, killing my appetite to shrink me, leading my thoughts up the rosy path of future love, to prepare me and make me strong for an uncertain future.

Everyone noticed my increasingly bony face and tightened belts. My sister asked, "Have you stopped eating, too?" My friend Rebecca, she of "eat the rat" fame, asked, "Do you find it ironic that as your husband's health declines, you're getting back in shape?" I waved away the comments, discouraged them. I didn't want to agree and thereby reveal myself to be the monster who took pride in her appearance when her husband was dying.

The one person who didn't comment on the change in my body was the man who knew it best. Granted, Glenn was drugged most of the time, and he was grappling with larger issues than my stomach bulge. When he was awake, we talked about anything, everything, no matter how small and insignificant. Glenn had always been a fantastic talker, a great gossip, which I appreciated so much in a man. We laughed about how some visitors to the Apartment Ward were undone by awkward attempts to act sufficiently reverent to the cancer patient. We theorized about our friends' relationships—how would they handle it if one of them got sick?—in minute detail. We strolled around the neighborhood, me pushing Glenn in the wheelchair, and gabbed about ugly clothes in shop windows, the high price of contact lens solution, a restaurant closing. We had lengthy conversations about Ben Stein and Jimmy Kimmel, the duo who hosted Glenn's favorite game show. We talked about us, and how great our lives would be once he recovered. We never talked about loss of life. Or loss of weight. And he didn't comment on my shrinking body, just as he hardly spoke of my expanding one.

With the perspective of years, I realize that my size, bigger or smaller, simply didn't register to him. Whatever it was he saw in me, it had nothing to do with my weight. If I had issued a subconscious test of his unconditional love by gaining weight, I hadn't been paying close enough attention to his marks. Glenn passed the test. He passed it over and over again, with flying colors. If I failed to see it then, I do now. And for that, I'm deeply grateful.

At the funeral, I wore a size ten ankle-length black skirt that Alison picked out for me. Everyone said I looked good, considering. Over the coming months, I continued to lose buckets of water weight through the tear ducts. The weight of guilt clung to me. I learned in my grief books that surviving spouses often feel guilt for being healthy, for not getting sick and dying.

My fantasies about having a happy—if distant—future were useful during the illness, but I had to put them away after the death. No matter how much I'd prepared for it, Glenn's absence from our home was shocking and huge. Maggie rightly said that her friends who'd lost grandparents couldn't understand. When you lose someone who lived in your house, you hurt more. You missed more. I felt like I'd lost, was lost, was left with loss. Losing—formerly the opposite of gaining—was now the antithesis of winning.

I spent night after night in a misery of loneliness and self-pity, alone in my bedroom with the TV on. This was the reality of widowhood. The fantasy had been a lot better. I had the sneaking suspicion I'd find those lost pounds again, probably sooner rather than later. And I feared that true love had vanished from my life forever.

5

SEX AND THE SKINNY

Myth or Fact? Fat girls . . .

1. Use their fat layer to hide from sex.
2. Are so hard up, they'll say yes to anyone—or anything.
3. Only do it in the dark.
4. Overeat because of sexual frustration.

Regarding Point #1, that fat girls hide from sex behind a layer of flab, I'd have to go with Fact. When I was a teenager, sex scared the hell out of me. I was intimidated by the physical intrusion. Learning to use tampons was traumatic enough. The emotional consequences seemed even worse. Based on my observations of girls who actually had a sex life, as soon as they put out, they were either dumped or gossiped about. "Slut" was not a sexually self-actualized term back in 1980s suburban New Jersey. As for how these girls *felt* about being sexually precocious, I came to this conclusion: More tears were spilled over having sex than over being a virgin. I decided

I would wait. Not that anyone was breaking down the door to get at me.

My libido simply hadn't kicked in. I didn't have explicit sexual fantasies, just fuzzy romantic ones. I didn't masturbate. I didn't have an orgasm until college. My sexual education—academic and anecdotal—was ridiculously inept. Everything I learned about teen sex was from movies like *The Last American Virgin* and *Fast Times at Ridgemont High*, with the themes of abortion, STDs, premature ejaculation, and betrayal. We all read Judy Blume's *Forever*, which starred a romantic hero who named his penis Ralph. *So* not a sexy name.

I had the physical maturity for lust, but not the will for it. I got crushes, safe ones on guys I barely knew, faces at assembly, bodies leaning against lockers in the hallways. The few times a boy hit on me at a keg party, I'd get so flustered, I'd break out in a flop sweat and retreat into the nearest bathroom to hide.

I believed, as bushmen in Africa do vis-à-vis photographs, that if I had sex with a boy, he'd steal my soul. So much of my dignity had been peeled away already, I was fiercely protective of the scraps I had left. Sex equaled vulnerability. Losing my virginity at seventeen had been an exercise in getting it over with. Emotionally, I felt nothing, during or afterward, except relief that the deed was done. I'd achieved my modest goal. I would not go to college a virgin.

I went to Dartmouth, a small college in New Hampshire where (it'd been said) the men were men, the women were men, and the sheep were nervous. As soon as I arrived on campus, I felt like an alien. A punk rock Jersey Jew who went to public school? I was like a rare endangered animal

among all those New England WASP boarding school prep-
pies. The preps of Short Hills were like babies learning to
crawl compared to the kids I met from Exeter, Andover, and
St. Paul's. They'd been shipped off to school, many of them,
at age thirteen, returning home only for holidays. I was in-
sanely jealous of them. I wished I'd been sent away!

These boarding school kids awed me. They were smarter,
wittier, and better educated than scrubs like me. One beautiful boy, E., a graduate of a New England prep school, en-
tranced me as if I were a cobra and he the charmer with a pot
pipe. He was also a "writer," and we spent hours in his dorm
room, listening to the Grateful Dead, having deep talks, and
passing the bong. E. had a red lightbulb in his desk lamp, and
it bathed his Indian blankets and Communist wall posters in
a seductive glow. We also shared short stories, what we considered "genius" snarls of prose scribbled in notebooks.

He was my first friend who was a boy. But our friendship
was also a lie. He thought we were having a meeting of
minds—and we were. I was madly in love with him, though,
and every second in his presence was an excruciating knife
twist of sexual longing. I wanted him, bad. The attraction
was visceral. My guts tightened when I was around him. I
wasn't sure if he knew. Some signs pointed to yes. He was an
exhibitionist and often removed his shirt, tried on another,
took that one off, and so on. He had the habit of rubbing his
palm in lazy circles over his taut tan belly and the down that
covered it. I asked him once if he realized he was doing it.
And by "it," I meant driving me insane with lust, inflaming
my urge to touch him, the craving for him to touch me. He
asked, "Doing what?"

We were best buds for a year. We talked and talked. Then, for a change of pace, we talked some more. We smoked pot, snorted coke, ate mushrooms, dropped acid. Somewhere in there, we took a few English lit classes together, read books, wrote angst-dripping short stories we'd show only to each other. His were often about his own sexual longings, which I fantasized were about me.

I didn't dare make a move. Although I finally understood what lust was, I hadn't a clue what to do about relieving it. I watched dozens of cute girls flow in and out of his life and bed. Each, in turn, complained to E. about me. They wanted to know why he gave his body to them but saved his soul for me. Of course, I would have gladly traded places with them, but at least I had the small pleasure of making the pretty girls jealous. Once or twice, E. told me that his girlfriend theorized that he was actually in love with me and didn't realize it. How we'd laugh and laugh at such an absurd notion. Thank God for the red lightbulb, or he'd have seen my cheeks glow.

After E. dumped a girl, the adorable, conical-breasted ex would seek me out. She'd show up at my dorm room, or track me down in the commons, and ask, "Where did I go wrong?" and cry about her loss. I could only imagine how hard it must have been, to get next to him, to be touched by his beautiful hands, and then abruptly be denied access. I sympathized, honestly. I tried to help the dumped girl, and gave sound and useful advice about moving on. But I had to go now, because I was meeting E. for dinner. My friendship with him, the consistency of it, was my revenge against the girls who got from him what I most wanted. True, I was the fat friend, not the girlfriend. That would have to satisfy, if nothing else did.

I *was* happy to be three hundred miles away from home. No one told me what to eat or do. I could smoke my cigarettes, pile my tray high at the cafeteria. I put on the freshman fifteen by midyear (at Dartmouth, it was called the Thayer Layer, named after the student dining hall). Maybe if I'd had a boyfriend instead of pining for E., I'd have burned the excess calories by having sex. Maybe I pigged out because I couldn't have E., but I could have dessert (see Point #4—fat girls overeat due to sexual frustration—also Fact).

I'd matured enough to handle the (confounding but consistent) sexual attention of other guys. A few times a month, I'd bring a guy back to my dorm room, have sex with him, and pretend to be asleep when he snuck out in the middle of the night. On the phone, my mother would ask if I was seeing anyone, and then she'd say, "Oh," when I told her I wasn't. I knew her "oh" was a truncated "I told you s-oh." Indeed, one of her main "reasons I want you to lose weight" was that boys didn't like dumpy girls. Her delivery system had been wrong, not to mention *loud,* and so was her message. A lot of boys did want me. Just not the ones I wanted.

My sexual interludes gave me grist for conversations with E. One sunny afternoon, we were sitting on rocks on the bank of the Connecticut River, talking about a boy I'd had a weeklong fling with. We'd driven out to the secluded spot to smoke a joint, watch the river flow, gaze at the green mountains in the distance. E. seemed distracted. He started rubbing my back and gave me the misty, half-lidded blue-eyed stare I'd seen him use on countless cuties.

He said, "I feel really close to you, Val."

I said, "That's nice. We should be getting back."

And then we got in the car and left that place—literally and figuratively—never to return.

It was my one and only opportunity. I'd been offered my heart's delight, in a romantic setting, and I refused. When I told my other friends what happened, I acted insulted. How dare E. try his cheesy seduction ploy on me—*me!*—the one girl who knew his soul. I was indignant, offended. The truth? I was a chicken. A coward. E. and I were outdoors, under the bright sun. In the two seconds between offer and refusal, I pictured that sun shining on my imperfections, E. seeing my body in unforgiving light and struggling not to recoil. On the silent drive back to campus, regret already settling in to stay, I hated myself for a whole new reason: I didn't have the guts to take what I wanted. I was so filled with disgust at my own cowardice, I could barely look at E. It got weird. We started to drift.

Looking back at that moment, as I have many times, I understand rationally that getting what I wanted was way outside my comfort zone. I had sex with guys I didn't care about. I cared about E. I'd always soothed my longing by telling myself sex with him would spell doom for our friendship. As it turned out, *not* having sex with him had the same result. I'd romanticized unrequited love. If love was requited, would it be nearly as exquisite? Was love equal to pain? And what, if anything, did this have to do with my relationship with my mother?

E. and I rediscovered each other by senior year. I was over him, sexually speaking. By then, I had a boyfriend of my

own. I met K. at the end of sophomore year. He would become my on-again, off-again boyfriend for the remainder of
my college career. K. and I started the usual way, a drug- and
alcohol-soaked one-night stand. We were at my place, an
off-campus apartment. K. was my roommate's friend. We had
our fling. Then I couldn't get rid of him. One night rolled
into another, and before I knew it, he was living with me. He
was a Dartmouth student, too, a senior on a year's personal-
ized curriculum. Every few months, he'd go on some kooky
trip tangentially related to his thesis research, driving
cross-country in a van or flying freight to Europe. His frequent travel was the reason it took him six years to graduate.
But it also made him seem mysterious and romantic—and
unavailable, which I was enthralled by.

My relationship with K. was all about drama. We fought
constantly, usually about how he was emotionally withhold-
ing. I'd throw a "You don't really love me" tantrum. He'd
take off on one of his trips. I'd break up with him and spiral
into Breakup Diets #1 through #17, during which time I
burned a lot of calories by having sex with his friends. I'd
beg K. to come back. When he returned, I'd confess about
all the guys I'd slept with, cry, and beg his forgiveness, he'd
accept my apology ("You're with me now," he said, filling
me with pride in his ownership), and we'd start the cycle
anew. Along the way, we'd smoke mountains of pot, talk
about philosophy, and listen to Bob Dylan. I respected his
intellect, and he would read anything I wrote. K. gave me
valid criticism. He made me question my ideas, and refused
to stroke my ego as E. and I had done for each other.

Although I was shy about getting on top with the lights

on (see Point #3—fat girls only do it in the dark—Partial Myth), I was bolder with K. than I'd been in my previous flings. He was a crunchy, organic, earthy guy. I thought of him as a mental giant, supercerebral, suspicious of superficial ideals of female pulchritude. He did tai chi. He meditated. He wore voluminous hippie clothing. "All bodies are beautiful," he said. I went with that.

For the record, at twenty, I was heavy. I'd adopted the Deadhead style of drawstring-waist baggy pants and peasant shirts that were one-size-fits-all. K. was slim and hairless. His body was beautiful, but I preferred the lights out and covers up whenever possible. He didn't object, so I assumed he'd rather not see my naked truth. He thought of sex as a mental/physical practice, like yoga or meditation. I wanted fiery passion, to feel ravaged by his uncontrollable lust. He wanted to gain insight into himself via sex with me.

Now, I realize our biggest problem was a clash of sexual styles. We should have broken up after two months. Instead, we limped along for over two years. I compulsively tried to seduce him—three, four times a day—to assure myself that my first and only boyfriend craved me desperately, or at least as desperately as I needed to feel craved. If he refused, I'd start a fight. Fights led to make-up sex, which temporarily quieted the insatiable beast within. But the victory was hollow. I knew I'd manipulated him into it.

There was no bliss in victory, either. Of the 300 sexual encounters we had, I faked orgasm 299 times.

No, that's an exaggeration. I faked 298 times.

Seriously, my faking depended on what we did. Certain

acts would guarantee an orgasm. Others were assured to fail. An honest estimate: I faked half the time.

Not K.'s fault. He was an experienced lover. He did what would have worked for any other woman (one who wasn't completely messed up about her body). And he rightly thought his techniques *were* working. I was a good faker. *Very* good. I served up Academy Award–winning performances, night after night. After a particularly nuanced display of my acting chops, as I lay next to him in bed, I wondered if I'd missed my calling, if I should've pursued a career on the stage.

As I later came to understand, bad body image and anorgasmia (not having an orgasm) went together like peanut butter and jelly. I came across this info while researching magazine articles: Two-thirds of American women have some degree of sexual dysfunction that is related to body image. One dysfunction is to think about their perceived body flaws during sex—fat thighs, for example—or to become fixated that their partner is turned off by the flaw. If women get locked in their heads during sex, their nerve endings fail to process the sensual stimulation. No processing, no progression along the sexual response cycle. They stall in the arousal phase, if they get that far, and fall way short of climax. Another common dysfunction is a behavior called "spectatoring." The anxious lover is so concerned about how she looks while having sex, she mentally watches herself doing it. In effect, she floats above her body, observing what's happening to her without actually feeling it.

A woman's feeling of attractiveness and desirability *defines* the quality of her sex life. Doesn't matter whether you're fat or not. What matters is that you *think* you're fat, during sex. Forget about having fun in bed. Forget about orgasms. Say hello to frustration, disappointment, guilt, and shame (incidentally, the same emotional hits triggered by diet cycling).

During sex with K., I was a spectator, mentally watching what was happening, as well as a thespian par excellence! I acted out the sexual rewards I wished I were having. I eventually told K. the truth, but not until I graduated and left Dartmouth. I was living in Cambridge, Massachusetts, to attend the Radcliffe Publishing Course, a summer program for aspiring editors and writers wanting to learn about the book and magazine business. K. came down from New Hampshire to visit me one weekend. We were broken up, but not completely severed. I remember sitting in my dorm room, him in a chair, me on the bed. It was early afternoon. The light came in through the window, illuminating the room in a calming way. He smiled at me with what appeared to be genuine trust, affection, pleasure in my company.

I said, "You know how I scream and thrash around in bed? I was kind of faking a little."

"A little?" he asked.

"A lot."

"You mean to tell me that for two years you've been lying to me?" he asked. "In the most personal way possible?"

"Not to be mean," I said. "I did it to be nice."

He was furious. Quickly, on the heels of that whopper, I told him that I was done with bedroom theatrics forever (indeed, I never faked again). To prove my point, I added that, just the other night, I screwed this Republican from the *Harvard Lampoon,* and I barely grunted for him. "For the record,"

I said, "I didn't find out he was a Republican until the morning after, and then I kicked his ass *out*."

Needless to say, K. was not reassured. He left Massachusetts within the hour. I called him a few days later, and he said, "For the rest of your life, no man will feel as comfortable with you as I did." That was his prediction and his curse. I believed it. The karmic boomerang of lying to K. would surely strike me right between the eyes. His words played into my deepest insecurities, those that he knew so well. I didn't deserve comfort. Trust wasn't feasible. I could never believe, beyond a shadow of a doubt, that any man would truly want me and love me.

The epilogue to the K. story: Shortly after 9/11, he tracked me down and called me in Brooklyn to make sure I was still alive. Life had taken him far. Postgraduation, he'd traveled the world and wandered for a decade. He'd finally settled down and was in law school in California. He was still single, but he sounded solid, happy. I told him my story, that my husband had died less than a year ago, and that I had nervously started to date again. He said, "Don't worry, Val. You're the whole package. Any guy would be lucky to have you." It was the nicest thing he'd ever said to me, at a time when I desperately needed to hear it. He lifted the curse.

During one of our extended breakups, the winter of my senior year at Dartmouth, K. left campus for a few months, and I moved into a house with several other students, one of whom was a coke dealer. The change of venue and free drugs made Breakup Diet #14 my greatest success yet. I dropped twenty-five pounds in two months. Thanks to my newly svelte body and a steady flow of traffic through our house (see above, re: coke dealer), I was deluged with sexual invitations. I accepted as many as I could.

If I were to chart my sexual activity along with my weight, the graph would show an inverse relationship. The smaller my pants, the bigger the number of men that got into them. One guy, a gorgeous just-a-friend from my sophomore dorm, saw me at a party and said he didn't recognize me at first. "You're just another pretty girl now," he said. I might have taken that the wrong way, but his hand was sliding deliciously down my back toward the curve of my ass. Men started to stammer when they spoke to me. They'd bring me beers and light my cigarettes. They tried to impress me with long boring stories about how they humiliated other men. They asked me to be their lucky charm at the pool table. When they said they'd be right back, they came right back. Several times, I realized with a start that two or three men were vying for my attention, clashing antlers over who'd get to take me home.

One of them surely did. That was guaranteed. The others would lash out. At me. That was the flip side of being an object of desire. If a woman gets rejected, she hates herself. If a man gets rejected, he hates the woman who turned him down. I flirted with one guy and then slipped away with another. The runner-up came by our house the next day, and pushed me hard into the refrigerator when I said I'd left the party with someone else. I juggled two friends, and circumstances led the three of us to have dinner together. During the main course, the guys fought over me like two lions over a scrap of meat. By dessert, they'd teamed up against me, accusing me of trying to ruin their friendship. They walked out on me. I'd started out with two guys and ended up with the bill.

Male desire became my drug of choice. Not *sex*. The sex itself was okay, sometimes good, sometimes awful, but being the object of lust became a new high, better than drugs or dieting. I got all the approval of being thin, all the ego boosting. I also got drinks, smokes, meals, strokes, jealous looks from conical-breasted blond girls. Having been so savagely negated as attractive by X., Y., and Z. as a teenager, I gobbled up the positive male attention of A., B., C., D., E., F., G., H., etc., like a starved animal. I embraced my sluttiude and made up for lost time. If a guy did me the favor of wanting me, I did him the favor of schtupping him. If my behavior was reckless, destructive, and soul-annihilating, I didn't see it. Or chose not to.

Friends, friends' brothers, colleagues. I racked up the numbers. A dozen in Europe during my semester abroad. Half a dozen my senior year at Dartmouth. Four of the seven male students at the Radcliffe course. Dozens of editorial assistant and junior editor types came in and out, as it were, of my first apartment in Brooklyn. I had a job, an income, my own place, much to prove, an unquenchable lust to be lusted after, and millions of New York City men at my disposal.

For the record, I had some standards. I didn't bed down with just anything. A guy had to be funny and smart. Cute. I had only one black ball: I wouldn't do fatties. A bitter rejection of my former fat self? You betcha. Superficial and hypocritical? To be sure. I knew it, too. It was right there, on the surface. Some of Mom's fatphobia had rubbed off on me.

Promiscuity went hand in hand (or *beep* in *beep*) with thinness. Counterintuitively, the more dinner dates I had, the less I ate. I sure did drink a lot, though. Vodka tonics were a staple of Sluttitude Diets #1 through #5. I had one-night stands, two-week flings, three-month affairs. Friends would say, "How's Bob?" And I'd say, "Bob who? I'm with Jim now." The dedication page of my second novel, *Murder on Wheels*, published at the height of my easy years, read: "Dedicated to Whomever I'm Seeing Right Now. Honey, You Know It's You." Which was supposed to be a joke but was also apt. I remember going to visit friends at the *Village Voice* offices, where I'd interned a few summers before. (Of course, I'd seduced one of the contributors, who was not there that day, whew.) My former boss, Karen, asked what was going on.

I said, "I'm seeing three guys."

She said, "Don't *brag*, Valerie."

I blinked at her, confused by the criticism. I hadn't thought I was bragging. I was just reporting the news. If I'd been asked what I had for breakfast, I'd have given as accurate and dispassionate a response.

"They'll probably dump me next week," I added humbly.

Guess what? All three *did* dump me. Despite my low weight and revolving bedroom door (see Point #2—fat girls will do anyone or anything—another Partial Myth), I was desperate and lonely—as well as hungry. Quickie relationships gave me a hit of the approval I was addicted to. I was in love with the approval, and, in my early twenties, I thought that meant I was also in love with the man. I lived in fear that I'd lose him, and as sure as chocolate has calories, my anxiety and nagging and demands for assurance would drive him away. Then I'd suffer, wail at the moon, call my friends hourly to give them the feelings update. I took scant pleasure in the relationship itself but was devastated when it ended.

Another of my mom's refrains had been "If you were thinner, you'd be happier."

Again, she was wrong. From age twenty-two to twenty-five, I had visible ribs. I ran miles and miles every day. My hipbones jutted. Yet I was chronically miserable, searching, searching, like a starved wild-eyed wolf in the woods, for love, some fucking (literally) relief from the loneliness and self-doubt.

Then I met Glenn, who saved me.

6

THAT'S RIGHT, I'M TALKING TO *YOU*

M e and the mirror. It's a hate-hate relationship. Doesn't matter if my weight is trending up or down. No matter what shape I'm in, I have a knack for finding the smallest physical flaws. It's a dark gift. One I can't give away.

I have my usual routine when approaching the mirror. I heavily sigh (exhaling makes the stomach flatter), tense my muscles, stand full-frontal before the glass (my most flattering angle), and then appraise. I give myself the once-over thrice. I slap my belly to see how much it jiggles. More than yesterday? Less? I pinch, poke, pull on the flab, and think, "Broiled Chicken Diet #12? . . . Nothing a few thousand crunches won't fix . . . You'll never lose it . . . worthless . . . pathetic . . . Maybe if I hire a trainer . . ." During one incredibly wiggly period a few years ago, I slapped the belly to check for jiggle nearly every hour. I realized how badly off I was when the rug between my desk chair and my closet mirror started to look frayed. One of the drawbacks of working from home.

After consulting a couple of experts and doing some light Googling, I discovered that I suffered from "appearance-checking behavior," or the habitual examination of one's perceived body flaws. Throw in the negative interior body talk, and you've got a bona fide compulsion.

My interior body talk echoed everything my mother ever said to me, plus some new material I came up with on my own. My subconscious playlist, hosted by DJ Inner Bitch, was automatic. The hits kept spinning, whether I heard them or not. "Fat . . . lazy . . . gross," the cerebral sound track of my life.

Perhaps the way to think positive would be to avoid mirrors and reflective surfaces, such as storefront windows, bathroom tile, car chrome, spoons, knives, clean plates, computer screens, framed pictures, windows, puddles, any calm water. I could live 24/7 in a squash court—or, more appropriately, a padded room in the psych ward.

Since my goal was to liberate myself from bad body image, I would have to tackle the mirror problem. I needed a practical approach. The emotional purging thus far had been productive. Crawling through bitter and lonely memories was unlocking a lot of stored-in-the-bones anger. Old rage seemed to be leaking from my pores. To speed the process, I'd been running on the treadmill like a fiend. *But*—in addition to the emotional release, I needed do some interior redesign of the brain. Move around the chairs in my mind. Repaint the skull walls. Break the appearance-checking habit.

As I devised a plan of action, I soon realized that gut slapping was part of a larger problem. My negative body talk didn't begin and end when I bellied up to the mirror. DJ Inner Bitch was in the house 24/7. She cranked out the hits when I looked at myself, but also when I daydreamed about having a flat stomach. When I got dressed. When I got undressed. When I compared myself unfavorably to other women. At meal time, sex time, all the time!

Since there was no accurate way to measure the emotional toll of near constant lambasting, I decided to take another approach. I *could* tally the cost in hours and minutes. I wasted precious time slamming myself. I certainly had better things to do than self-annihilation. Perhaps if I figured out how much of my day-to-day life was lost on negative thought, the terrible truth would spur my conscious mind to overcome my undermining subconscious.

The next day, I bought a stopwatch.

Within a couple of hours, though, I realized my methodology was faulty. When a thought became conscious, the stream didn't flow. I'd focus more on having the thought than on the thought itself, interrupting its duration. Also, I wasn't clear on which thoughts should count toward the total. Choosing a snack? Organizing my day around going to the gym? My thoughts rarely lasted a full minute. Often, I'd have a fat flash (for example, intense envy about how skinny Norah Jones looked on her new CD cover), but it was too fleeting to measure. The flash would end before I had a chance to start the stopwatch.

I had to refine my strategy, think in terms of "instances"

rather than "instants." If I could get a baseline of negative thoughts, I could mindfully decrease them.

The next day, I bought a clicker.

On Monday, I looked at myself 166 times. About ten times per waking hour, or, on average, once every six minutes. Shocking, isn't it? I mentioned the number to friends, and they gasped. The huge total included home mirror visits and catching my reflection in storefront windows, car windows, any chrome or glass surface. I counted everything, even fleeting glimpses if they were long enough to judge myself. The gym is a riot of mirrors. I logged twenty separate instances in an hour of watching myself sweat.

What was even more appalling? Every instance of looking at myself was accompanied by a negative thought. As I already knew, the thought could be fleeting, as long as it took the idea or word "hefty" to flit across my mind. I wanted raw data on how often I had negative thoughts in total, not *only* when looking at myself. I knew cluing into my subconscious would be a challenge. I resolved to try.

On Tuesday, I put the clicker to use counting each instance of negative thought. A flash, a microflash. Since one thought could roll into the next, I wasn't sure if it was one long thought or a series of thoughts that should be counted separately. I decided to apply the logic of multiple orgasm to multiple negative thoughts: If there was a thirty-second break between thoughts, they were to be tallied separately. If one thought led instantaneously into the next (as in, "jeans too bloody tight . . . embarrassment . . . shame . . . that woman's jeans look great . . . she probably eats grilled radicchio," so on and so forth), I'd count it as one solid click.

As it happened, on Tuesday, an unexpectedly warm day, I had to take off my hoodie while doing errands and walk around in a snug T-shirt. I was exceedingly self-conscious about back bacon and the muffin top. If I'd worn yoga pants and a peasant shirt . . . well, no point mitigating the shocking truth. I clicked 263 distinct instances of negative thought on that one day, including random barbs and assessments while looking at myself. I was sure I missed flashes that were too quick, or too deep in the subconscious, to access.

Calculators out: Two hundred and sixty-three hits divided by sixteen waking hours equaled sixteen and a half hits per hour. Or one hit *every three and a half minutes.*

Even on her energetic days, Mom wasn't that relentless.

Imagine what it'd be like to pinch yourself every three and a half minutes.

This was far, far worse than a sharp stick in the eye.

I was my own worst enemy; I was a formidable foe. How on earth could I liberate myself from bad body image when negative thoughts were the glue that held my subconscious together? I wondered what else I thought about. For the next few days, I tallied the rising thought bubbles about other matters.

On Wednesday, I thought about sex thirty-four times.

On Thursday, I thought about my family eighty-seven times.

On Friday, I thought about my work ninety-eight times.

On Saturday, I thought about money sixty-six times.

Looking at the week's raw data, I resisted ranking my priorities according to how often I thought about the subject.

Obviously, I'd be more preoccupied with my family if we were in crisis, but on Thursday, we stuck flawlessly to the usual routine without incident. Regarding the work total, I counted random thoughts during nonworking hours. Obviously, while working, I thought about what I was doing. Family and work thoughts tended to be logistical and practical, not critical or negative. Money thoughts were usually crunching numbers in my head, adding and subtracting, sometimes worrying. Sex thoughts were surprisingly fleeting, such as admiring my husband, Steve, in his new jeans, and thinking they'd look even better on the floor. No lurid daydreams on that busy Wednesday.

The cumulative four-day total of thoughts about sex, family, work, and money was only a bit higher than my one-day total of negative body image blips. This experiment reminded me of Scared Straight videos in high school about drunk driving and the clap. I was horrified and depressed, hating my subconscious. On Sunday, I tallied my negative thoughts about how often I have negative thoughts: 176.

I would never win the body image battle unless I recalibrated my brain, or "did some unlearning," as Susanna, my Krishnamurti-loving former roommate, used to say.

I would become my own thought police, determined to improve my numbers. If I could make a positive turn, logic would have it that my outlook and attitude, generally speaking, would lift.

Redirecting thought was surprisingly easy to do. When I felt compelled to run the hourly check for miraculous deflation of my stomach bulge, I took a deep breath, rooted myself in my desk chair, and played Snood on the computer until the urge passed. When I walked down the street, I'd strap on a set of imaginary blinders, keeping my eyes front and center, thereby avoiding my reflection in car and storefront windows. After a few days, I routinely managed to redirect my gaze—and my thoughts.

Not racking up scores of bad body image thoughts created a vacuum in my mind that desperately, achingly, needed to be filled. Wish I could say a wave of deep philosophical thoughts flooded my brain. Or that I was suddenly drowning in brilliant ideas for novels. To fill the mental hole, as it were, I thought about sex. Day and night. Afternoon and evening. Acts. Positions. Fantasies. What I'd like to do, what I wanted Steve to do to me, and how all that could be physically feasible given the limitations of human anatomy. Thoughts inspired action. Steve didn't know what hit me—or, more accurately, what hit *him*. Not that he was complaining. I was aware that I'd probably replaced one obsessive thought pattern with another, but this felt healthier and far more satisfying.

I wondered if orgasmic relief was the emotional lift I'd been anticipating. It was certainly physically uplifting. Emotionally? Sure! I kept on my imaginary blinders, avoided extraneous mirror use, consciously and subconsciously replaced negative body thoughts with erotic ones. And all was good.

Then it happened. After a month of waiting, the epiphany came unexpectedly. I was walking Lucy home from school. We passed a huge store window by a pharmacy. I used to slow down at that place on the sidewalk to check my profile view in the glass. For weeks now, I'd been intent on looking straight ahead, to avoid the reflection, but on that day, my eyes wandered a bit. I turned them downward, looking at Lucy as she told me a story about school in her eight-year-old excitable way. When she noticed I was looking at her—not at the window, not straight ahead—she smiled up at me, big and beautiful. Looking at her gorgeous face (she is one spectacular kid), I was overcome with gratitude for her being my daughter, for how innately happy she was, how animated and full of life and joy. We locked eyes; energy passed between us. It was no ordinary look. No ordinary connection.

How many of those moments had I missed while frowning at my profile in storefront windows? For years—decades—I'd been mentally trashing myself, obsessing about myself, when the beauty and glory of life was outside of me, my thoughts, my body. It was a horrible, shameful feeling, realizing that myopia and critical self-absorption had defined my existence for quite some time. Worse, my kids had probably noticed.

Naturally, I fell into a spell of myopia and critical self-absorption about the fact that I'd been myopic and . . . you see where this is going.

The time had come to step back, or think in reverse, and ask broader questions of myself, such as "What is the point? Why am I doing this?" One could cut to the heart of existentialism in front of a mirror. Lock in on the eyes—not the stomach, or the thighs—and make a vow to yourself to define existence by generating thoughts, feelings, and actions that increase the amount of joy and happiness in your head, your home, and the world.

Yes, counting negative thoughts on a clicker had come to this. I'd found the big idea, and I aspired to live by it from that moment on the street with Lucy forever forward. Simply put, I wanted to be a better person. And that, as I understood it, had *absolutely nothing* to do with the bulge of my belly.

7

UGLY VALERIE

At twenty-four, in the throbbing throes of my slut years, I was fired from my first magazine job as a fact-checker. At the time, I had a tenuous grasp on what constituted a "fact." My six-month unemployment was a low weight period. Nerves diminished my appetite. In the yawning absence of stuff to do, I went running every day. I also looked for jobs. I went to an interview at *Mademoiselle* magazine for an associate editor position. The fifty-year-old Condé Nast staple had a hallowed history. Alumni included Joan Didion, Truman Capote, Sylvia Plath, and Mary Cantwell. The annual short fiction contest was legendary. I wanted this job. I needed it. I was never going to get it.

I'd interviewed at *Mademoiselle* two years before. That job was beauty and fitness writing. I guess I wasn't beautiful or fit enough. I didn't make it to the short list. This second interview was set up by a friend from my fact-checking job. It was a courtesy interview, a foot in a door that would otherwise have been slammed in my face. I had zero editing experience. My magazine clips were more like long captions than actual articles. I must have put on a good show nonetheless (perhaps I was so convinced it wasn't going to happen, I didn't come off as desperate). I was offered the job and snatched it up before the bosses had the chance to come to their senses.

Thus far, my life had been gender mixed. Working at *Mademoiselle* was like entering the Female Zone, a no-man's-land (make that no-*straight*-man's-land) where every insecurity was magnified under the constant scrutiny of peers. If I thought body size mattered in junior high school and at home, I hadn't seen nothin' yet.

On my very first day, I realized that the magazine was not on solid footing. Before I'd been shown to my desk, I heard hallway rumors that the editor-in-chief, Amy Levin Cooper, was going to be fired any day. I was told by my assistant (incredibly, I shared a coffee-fetch girl with two other editors) that the magazine's circulation and ad page numbers were down, and that Cooper was holding on by a zebra-print silken thread to the job she'd held for a decade. In those days, the powers that be at Condé Nast were infamous for unceremoniously sacking editor-in-chiefs and replacing them with spanking new buzz-worthy versions. The best-known example was *Vogue* editor Grace Mirabella learning she was being replaced by Anna Wintour while watching the TV news. Traditionally, the incoming editor cleaned house, firing the old staffers one by one (so as not to appear ruthless) and bringing in her own people. If Amy Levin Cooper were canned, the new editor, whoever she was, would fry my ass before she'd finished her morning cappuccino. The rumors made the office environment palpably tense. Tension brought desperation. In pitch meetings, we frantically grasped for big, splashy ideas. What grabby cover story, we wondered, would hold off Cooper's axing for one more month?

The articles department consisted of half a dozen editors and several assistants—all women in their midtwenties to early thirties. The articles head, M., the woman who hired me, was the oldest, at thirty-five. As a department, we were to supply the magazine with about sixty pages of original editorial content for every issue. When pitching feature articles, we stuck to the three *D*'s—dieting, dating, and diseases of the gynecological variety, as in, "My vaginal discharge smells funny. Help!" We ran arts reviews, advice columns, horoscopes, and celebrity profiles. Also, we'd do the monthly topical feature about a women's issue (rape, abortion, sexual harassment, etc.). At *Mademoiselle,* I learned that women's hot-button political issues were always about the control and protection of our bodies.

The ultimate juicy "get" article was a content trifecta that combined dieting, disease, *and* politics: the eating disorder first-person essay or reported investigation of a clinic that served the emergent needs of the self-starved or self-emetic. Every editorial pitch meeting, we'd collectively rack our brains for a new eating-disorder-of-the-month article.

According to available data, 1 percent of young women are anorexic, 2 percent are bulimic, and 5 percent are chronic bingers (by far the most prevalent eating disorder in America). All other disorders are subcategories of the big three. (Imagine my astonishment when I learned that my bent, chronic dieting, was a subcategory of anorexia! I thought, "If only I could have full-blown anorexia for, like, a month."

Alas, I'd had the JV version for, like, a decade.) It didn't matter that relatively few of *Mademoiselle*'s three million readers actually suffered from life-threatening food-related illnesses. You didn't need to have an eating disorder to feel fascination, disgust, and sympathy for those who did. An anorexic strapped down to a hospital bed for intravenous force-feeding? A bulimic's first purge memory from summer camp or a sorority hazing ritual? The readers lapped it up like pudding. They took these stories as cautionary tales of a run-of-the-mill obsession with thinness taken to horrifying extremes.

In those pre-Google days, we relied on press releases, books, medical newsletters, health studies, and regional newspaper articles to find subjects. Or we'd dip into the vast reservoir of our friends, friends-of-friends, cousins-of-friends, friends-of-cousins. When that well ran dry, we needed only to turn to ourselves. Of the dozen-odd women in the articles department, three-quarters of us had some kind of eating quirk or habit that any shrink alive would diagnose as borderline pathological. We beat national eating disorder statistical averages in a landslide. One assistant ate only a bunch of green grapes and six jelly beans every day. Another traveled with a food scale and weighed every morsel, even at restaurants. Another took twice-daily laxative-tea and high-volume-defecation breaks. Another was a diet product aficionado, swallowing any pill, drink, or bar she could get her hands on (and she got her hands on *everything;* huge shipments of products arrived weekly from companies looking for a mention in the magazine). Still another editor was an exercise-aholic, sweating out hours of her spare time on the StairMaster. A copy editor had full-blown anorexia, which she wrote an essay about in the magazine. A beauty writer was a full-blown binger, which she wrote an essay about in the magazine. We did an article once on what it was like to be really, really fat in America. The model we used looked huge to us, but when the issue came out, readers sent in letters complaining that the woman in the pictures wasn't nearly fat *enough*. She was normal, they wrote. At *Mademoiselle,* we didn't know from normal.

My chronic dieting went to extremes at *Mademoiselle.* There was tremendous pressure to look the part, or, as hires were told by the human resources staff, to represent the magazine in our personal appearance. Our work ethic: Get thin or die trying (the irony was particularly acute while editing stories about girls who *had* died trying). I certainly quaffed my share of chromium picolinate and Dexedrine. I munched bags of newfangled diarrhea-inducing Olestra-loaded potato chips ("shit chips" we called them). To further stimulate the bowels and curb appetite, I snorted white hillocks of cocaine. I did more blow during my first two years at *Mademoiselle* than in college when I lived with a coke dealer. I would snort before work, after work, and, occasionally, at work. My eyes would start popping, my heart rate zooming, and I'd crank out a story on first-date deal breakers.

If it hadn't been for the blow, I never would've been able to get to and stay at a size eight. Even at that weight, I was the biggest girl in the articles department. I felt acutely self-conscious about my curves. I was sure my job was on the line because I had them. Thinness was just one more way to win favor with the bosses, one more measure of success. It almost didn't matter if I edited twenty pages an issue. The skinniest girls on staff could edit five and get more approval from M., the boss. M. herself was slim but gawky, a former food writer who praised a gourmand lifestyle out of one side of her mouth and trashed her staff for being fat out of the other. With my own ears, I heard her rail against other editors' bodies, hair, clothes, intelligence, tone of voice. When I wasn't around, she gossiped about me to others, brutally mocking my CP Shades clothes and big boobs. Her alleged epithet for me was "the frizzy-haired fat Jew."

I didn't care about the "frizzy-haired" part or the "Jew" part (they were redundant). M. was from a large southwestern state. She'd met maybe two Jews before she moved to New York and was suddenly surrounded by them (us), including Ms. Levin Cooper. I forgave M. her bigotry. But the "fat" comment bothered me. After all, my job hung on my body size. Career advancement ran on a parallel track with weight reduction. If she considered me fat when I was at a low-for-me 130 pounds, what chance did I have in this business?

As a child, I'd equated slimness with approval and love. As an adult, thinness meant career survival.

Granted, the pressure on the articles department at *Mademoiselle* wasn't nearly as bad as it was on the fashion department. We were word people—supposedly, the brainy girls on staff. Unlike the fashion and beauty teams, articles editors were cut *some* slack about their appearance. But skinny mattered, from the top of the masthead to the lowest ranking assistant (*The Devil Eats Nada?*). I watched from a distance as Cooper, already tiny, got smaller as the rumors of her firing flared up, cooled, reheated, cooled again. An articles editor's fiancé bolted at the altar, and she started scarfing laxatives. Another's father committed suicide; she stopped eating sugar. And bread. And meat. Focusing on weight was a convenient substitute when one's real problems were too big or painful to deal with. For most of the Cooper era at *Mademoiselle,* I was sleeping around, getting dumped, doing dangerous drugs, smoking over a pack a day. Yet I never contemplated the skankiness of my life, or the bleak future that awaited me if I didn't change my ways. Instead, I thought about the number of calories in a tablespoon of diet salad dressing.

An even bigger distraction than weight? Hunger. Back then, we editors were all hungry for job security, advancement, success. We were also hungry for food. Self-starvation was a competitive sport. At staff lunches, the girl who ate the least won. I can't count how often editors would announce, after taking three bites of a sandwich, "Oh, God, I'm absolutely *stuffed.* I couldn't *possibly* eat another bite." Then, in classic control-freak fashion, they'd leave the barely dented sandwich on their desk all day long like a badge of honor, as in, "Look at what I *didn't* eat today!" When we had birthday parties in the office, slices of cake on paper plates would languish on the conference room table untouched (except by that one binger). During downtime, we'd sit in our offices smoking cigarette after cigarette (to quell hunger) and talking for *hours* about who ate what, the calorie counts of our lunches, the latest dieting trends, who on staff looked heavy, who looked thin, what we'd love to weigh, and then, contrarily, how stupid it was to obsess about food and weight when there were so many other, more important things to talk about.

Weight was our world. We couldn't escape it. Even the

staffers with relatively healthy attitudes about food kept a close eye on the expanding and deflating asses on parade in the hallways. It was relentless, the fat talk. Just like home. The editors, my friends, were like a battalion of fatphobic mothers, but younger and better dressed.

Every six months or so, a news story would come across the transom ("heroin chic," for example) and accuse women's magazines of fostering an unhealthy ideal of beauty that no ordinary woman could hope to attain. Were we to blame for eating disorders and drug abuse? Was it our fault designers made clothes the average woman couldn't fit into? Had we created a cultural environment where 99 percent of women had some degree of dissatisfaction with their appearance?

To defend my occupation, I told people, "I don't see how you can go from a pretty picture in a magazine to a girl sticking her finger down her throat." I still believe that there are just too many steps between being born and wanting to kill yourself to lay the blame solely on the media. Editors could certainly attempt to widen the lens of what's considered beautiful. Even slightly. Instead of showing size two models exclusively, editors could shove a size four or six into a bathing-suit fashion spread. You know, in the back row or hiding behind a palm tree.

Speaking of models, six-foot-tall, pencil-thin blonds wandered through the hallways at *Mademoiselle* regularly. We always knew when the fashion department was holding auditions because the reception area filled with refugees from Planet Barbie.

Paradoxically, a particular model kept my body image from sinking all the way into oblivion. One myth that magazines *do* perpetuate is that any woman, given time on the treadmill, beauty treatments, and flattering clothes, can achieve model gorgeousness. I bought that myth completely and blamed myself for failing to come close. Then I met Cindy Crawford. I got to stare at her for two hours while interviewing her for a *Mademoiselle* cover story. She laughed, smiled, was serious, contemplative, bemused, skeptical. No matter her expression, Crawford was—is—unspeakably, dumbfoundingly, jaw-droppingly gorgeous. Otherworldly gorgeous. Not-of-this-species gorgeous. I could lose half my weight, exercise until my brain turned to muscle, and get total face and body plastic surgery, and I would never approach her degree of beauty. Meeting Cindy Crawford made a realist out of me. I stopped comparing myself to models and movie stars. But comparing myself unfavorably to my peers? Business as usual.

After two years at *Mademoiselle,* things took a nasty turn. Cooper started to feel extreme pressure from above to revitalize the magazine. If the layouts were found lacking, a human sacrifice was made in the art department. The fashion was stale? Good-bye, fashion director. An article fell flat? Sayonara, editor. Heads rolled with Henry VIII regularity. It seemed like a colleague quit (fled) or was fired every couple of weeks. When a pregnant editor packed up for maternity leave, vowing never to return, I realized I hadn't a friend left on staff. I should've been applying for other jobs, but my morale and confidence were snake-belly low. I thought I was untalented, useless, inept, but mainly way too fucking *fat* to get hired at another magazine.

M. moved me to the top of the human sacrifice list and

launched a campaign to get rid of me. She sabotaged my work, trashed me in meetings, scorned my frizzy-haired fat Jewishness. Little did she know that I was highly skilled in the art of taking it. My ability to withstand verbal punishment was heralded far and wide (see previous chapters, all of them). M. was tough, but she couldn't hold a candle to X., Y., and Z. Her harsh treatment had reduced other editors to shattered waifs who locked themselves in bathroom stalls to cry. It left me unscathed. Seemingly. Just as in junior high, I appeared unaffected on the outside, but a tempest roiled within. I cried plenty, believe me, in my apartment. At the office, I was dry eyed and stiff lipped.

I could only imagine how frustrating my apparent placidity must have been to M. She used every weapon she had—glaring at me savagely in the halls, writing cruel remarks on pieces I wrote, killing articles I'd edited—but she couldn't break me. The rest of the staff pitied me, but I think they envied my ability to stay cool under fire. Of course, I wasn't *really* cool. I hated M. with a white-hot volcanic fury. I knew her treatment was unfair, but on some level, I felt it was inevitable. I'd been afraid of getting fired since day one. I was, after all, the largest editor in the department. I had the least fashionable clothes, the frizziest hair. I didn't belong.

As it came to pass, I outlasted both M. and Cooper. The rumors finally came true. Cooper was out. The incoming editor, Gabé Doppelt, a South African sprite and a former fashion editor at *Vogue,* dispatched M. and, eventually, every other editor in the department—except me. To this day, I have no idea why Doppelt kept me around. In gratitude, I worked my ass off for her. She was stylish, smart, and funny—plus, she had that accent. I desperately wanted to please her. As per her vision, we turned Cooper's perky college-girl magazine into a grunge-era bible of cool. *Mademoiselle* was suddenly relevant. As the magazine's hot factor rose, so did my self-esteem. As I regained my confidence, I improved my skills, met new people, relaxed into the environment of acceptance and positive reinforcement.

Doppelt hired a few male editors. The Female Zone was suddenly co-ed. We worked long hours; we ate meals together daily, sometimes on weekends. Dieting, food, and weight talk were replaced with gabbing about bands, movies, the war in Yugoslavia, Russian brides, the burgeoning Internet. We lingered over lunches. We munched on brownies at meetings. Birthday party cakes were devoured. We ordered calorie-dense takeout dinners. I barely registered who ate what, or what I ate.

I started gaining—but it didn't appear to matter. At the new *Mademoiselle,* we were judged on our ideas, not our waist-to-hip ratio. It was a dizzying shift. I was happy, satisfied, engaged to be married. For a wedding gift, Doppelt bought Glenn and me way too many items off our registry, and she sent me an enormous bouquet of peonies that made the entire floor smell great. I felt valued and appreciated, which stimulated my appetite for work, praise—and cheeseburgers.

I'll always be grateful to Doppelt for rebuilding my eroded confidence. Unfortunately, she didn't last long at *Mademoiselle.* Like Cooper, she got a lot of pressure from above. Unlike Cooper, Doppelt refused to sacrifice her staff to save herself. After one year as editor, she quit.

Elizabeth Crow would take over leadership of the magazine. A lioness of a woman, Elizabeth was oversized in personality and stature. Under her leadership, *Mademoiselle* tripled in circulation and doubled its page count. With her bottomless energy, enthusiasm, and experience, Elizabeth turned her staff, including me, into worshipful followers of her vision. She believed that young American women were smart and creative, but they could still use a little help with the details of life. That was my operating directive for the seven years I worked with Elizabeth, the most gratifying years of my professional life. If Cooper concerned herself with style, and Doppelt cared about cool, Elizabeth focused on the heart and soul of her readers, and her staff.

My heart had been battered. My soul needed nurturing. Every day at work was like a spa treatment for the spirit. *Mademoiselle* was finally the dream job I'd always hoped it would be. During the Elizabeth years, I had two children, wrote five books, came of age.

I also gained forty pounds, which mitigated the happiness considerably.

8

REAL BUTTER

Diet junkies think of certain foods as "bad" and "evil," equating an inert lump of sugar, fat, and carbs with terrorists and murderers. Putting "cupcake" in the same category as "Osama bin Laden" is just wrong. Yet millions of women do it a dozen times a day. The negative associations with food override the pleasure one derives from eating it. Consider the innocent square of chocolate. A chronic dieter would behold said square and mentally veer from "love" to "loathe" in a nanosecond. If she were to pop it into her mouth, thoughts and feelings would careen around her brain at lightning speed: "Unh, yummy . . . sweet . . . rich . . . fattening . . . a second on the lips, a century on the hips . . . the guilt . . . the shame . . . I have no willpower . . . I suck . . ."

Eating, every bite, becomes an emotional conflict.

The psychological term for this ricochet of conflicted thought is "restrained eating." The phrase might sound benign, but it refers to an insidious tendency to agonize over every bite, even when these bites are coming in rapid succession, at dizzying speed, while standing in front of an open refrigerator. In fact, one might say that the agony over every mouthful fuels the craving for the next bite, and so it goes.

As well as being a chronic dieter, with appearance-checking behavior, I was also a restrained eater. In essence, I'd been eating anxiety for thirty years. Any doctor would tell you: That can't be good for the heart—or the soul.

My friend Nancy is a talented amateur chef. For one of our monthly dinner/card-game nights with two other friends, Nancy prepared an incredible meal of fresh pasta with home-made sauce, salad, and apple raspberry crumble. While we were eating, I asked her what made her sauce so delectable.

"I stew the tomatoes and paste with pork fat," said Nancy.

Pause to picture me, fork hovering just outside my mouth, the piece of pasta upon it suddenly sprouting devil horns and a tail.

Nancy watched me react. "Just eat it, Val," she said. "A little pork fat won't kill you."

Oh, I ate it, all right. Loving/loathing every savory bite. The apple crumble was superb, too. One of the other card players asked for Nancy's secret ingredients for this dish. "Real butter," said Nancy, looking at me, daring me to react. "And real sugar. Which won't kill you either, Val."

Ever the journalist, I decided to investigate Nancy's bold claim. According to the Department of Health, there was not a single incident of death by apple crumble in the United States in the last decade. A one-time use of pork fat in pasta sauce had not claimed the life of a single American citizen.

Nonetheless, in my never-ending pursuit of substituting chemical food product (my *especialité*) for real, whole food (Chef Nancy cuisine), I set out to reproduce Nancy's apple crumble using my own ingredients. I broke out the Smart Balance tub, the Splenda box, and the low-carb flour and baked. When the dessert came out of the oven, it smelled and looked pretty good. Not *as* good, of course, since Splenda doesn't melt crispy like real sugar, and Smart Balance spread doesn't caramelize the apples like real butter. I served it to the fam. My husband and daughters gave me dutiful applause. It was fine . . . but it didn't come close to Nancy's version.

A few months ago, I would have crowed about my accomplishment of replicating real food successfully. I would've felt proud to have sold myself and my family on a subpar dessert. But this "apple crumble" left a bad taste in my mouth. Was my dish really more virtuous and "good" than Nancy's? From a taste perspective, hell no. From an emotional perspective? I realized (aha moment, coming up) that using substitutes was not emotionally healthy. It perpetuated the negative thinking I was trying to break free of. Sugar was not an Osama bin Laden. Butter was not a Kim Jong-Il. I shouldn't be afraid of them.

To eat like an emotionally healthy person, I would have to separate food and fear. Butter shouldn't raise my internal terror alert to orange. I had to embrace it. Take a long luxurious swim in a bath of it. I resolved to associate food with pleasure only and ditch the anxiety.

It would be an adjustment. One forkful at a time. I could pinch myself whenever I thought of food in a negative way. I could break out my clicker (dear old friend!) and count how often I had fearful food thoughts. Instead, I went with a positive approach: to retrieve sense memories of eating for pleasure. Surely there had been a few times in my life when a meal had all the emotional flavor of real butter, whole milk, and raw sugar. Five meals sprang to mind . . .

1. I WAS TWENTY-FIVE YEARS OLD, recently dumped, recently fired, living in a dilapidated apartment in Park Slope, Brooklyn, with two other people. I was running out of money and desperate to find a job, and the manuscript for my first novel had been rejected by twelve publishers. I spent many afternoons sitting in the window, strumming my guitar, singing "Knocking on Heaven's Door" over and over again, watching the hooker who lived on the corner walk up and down the street in her spandex dress. The bright sun made the guitar feel warm in my hands. I played on.

Then the phone rang. It was my agent. The thirteenth publisher wanted to buy my book.

The world turned upside down. The future cracked open. I started shaking. My vision crystallized, and my crappy apartment suddenly looked like a palace. In the span of thirty seconds, I registered a seismic shift of the soul. No matter what was to come, for the rest of my life, I would be an author.

I called my parents first. My mother had always been a staunch supporter of my writing. When I was in second grade, I wrote a poem about love—on construction paper I'd cut into the shape of a heart—that she thought worthy of publication. Anyway, my parents were excited by the news.

Probably relieved, too. Mom gushed on the phone. Dad was almost too proud to speak. They might've been happier for me than I was for myself. Now that I'm a parent, I get that. I can't imagine the immeasurable joy I'll feel when Maggie's and Lucy's dreams come true.

My roommate Susanna soon came home from work, and I told her what happened. She knew how low I'd been lately, and the good news inspired her to scream and throw her arms around me. We jumped up and down together in the living room and then went to the supermarket. I spent almost all the cash I had left on groceries, cheap stuff, box pasta, jar sauce, seven-dollar bottle of red wine. We cooked an absurd amount of spaghetti and baked loaves of garlic bread, swilled the wine, ate until we nearly puked. We celebrated with food and drink, as people had since troglodytes dragged bleeding carcasses back to their caves. As I fell asleep/passed out later, I knew it had been a day, a night, and a meal I'd remember forever.

2. **TWO YEARS LATER, GLENN AND I WERE A COUPLE.** We'd been together for nearly a year, but we had yet to go out for a superfancy meal together. The opportunity arose when, as a reward for busting my ass on a big special project for *Mademoiselle,* my boss offered to pay for a dinner for two, anywhere in New York City. Bouley in Tribeca was, at the time, the most expensive and highest-rated restaurant in Manhattan. I called and made a reservation for the night of my twenty-seventh birthday.

It was a big night for us. We dressed up at his apartment on the Upper West Side. I borrowed a size six black velvet dress from his roommate. It was snug, but I was determined to wear it. I also wore patent pumps, black stockings, and a garter belt. The outfit looked great standing up. Seated, the dress dug into my waist and rode up my thighs, revealing my garter belt straps. I had to tug at the hem all night to keep from flashing my lingerie at anyone who glanced in our direction. In spite of my fidgeting, Glenn grinned at me bashfully as if I'd stepped off the pages of a Victoria's Secret catalog. He was treating our extravagant night out with such sincere gallantry, I was charmed, touched, reminded that in this relationship I could leave my cynicism at home and let myself adore and be adored.

We took in the country French decor, the low candlelight, the three waiters per table. I'd been to four-star restaurants with my parents, but this was a dating first. It felt like we were playing grown-up. When Glenn ordered a fifty-dollar bottle of wine (the second least expensive on the list) and the waiter said, "Excellent choice," we started laughing at the surreality of our being there at all.

As advised by a foodie friend, we ordered the prix-fixe menu, a sampling of twelve tiny courses. The waiters would descend on us with each course, depositing a gorgeous dish before us, explaining in exquisite detail how chef David Bouley had hand-selected this prawn, lovingly, artfully grilled it, whisked the ingredient-packed sauce, wept tears of pride while plating it. We were encouraged to try a certain wine with the fish, another with the beef. Just when we thought the sensory overload might blind and cripple us, we dug deep to make room for more deliciousness to come. The whole time—a four-hour meal—Glenn and I talked about us. How we met. How much fun we'd had so far. How well our lives meshed. Like the food, Glenn and I were comprised of distinct flavors that, when combined, were complementary and harmonic, as if Bouley himself had hand-selected us to blend together.

This was serious romance—rich, heady, and indulgent. By the first of three dessert courses, my dress was incredibly tight around the gut. I'd given up tugging down the hem, and my stocking tops were plainly visible. We were both pretty drunk, too, on our third bottle of wine. Glenn reached into his pocket and withdrew an oblong jewelry box. My first thought was that it had to be a watch. I'd asked for one, after all. He handed it to me and said, "Happy birthday."

I opened the box. Not a watch. In the center of the velvet pillow sat a diamond ring. Underneath that, a label strip with the typed words: "If you've got the time, I've got the years. Marry me, Val."

The honest truth was that I'd kind of seen the proposal coming. There'd been a lot of buildup to this night, a month of anticipation. But even if I'd expected a proposal, I hadn't prepared for it. The waiters hovered nearby. The couples on either side of us were watching. I tried on the ring, which was way too small, and felt touched that Glenn thought my fingers were that bony and delicate.

Glenn was a true romantic, a sap, the kind of guy who wanted everything to be perfect. When we left the restaurant, the last truffle consumed, the huge bill paid with a corporate card, he surprised me again. He announced that he'd taken a room at the Empire Hotel, and his roommate had dropped off overnight bags for us, now waiting in the coat room. Along with clothes and toiletries, Glenn had packed a CD of Frank Sinatra love songs to play in our room on our engagement night.

We stumbled onto the street. The streetlights, once flat and white, now glowed golden. The formerly dirty, dark street had turned slick, shiny, glimmering. Glenn kept a protective arm around his drunk, high-heeled, excruciatingly tight-dressed fiancée while he hailed a taxi. As out-of-body happy as I was, I also felt dangerously overstuffed. I feared the dress would burst open. But I didn't care. My *life* had just burst open, in a dizzying array of flavors. And I knew that our engagement meal had been a sample, just a taste, of the wonders of our life yet to come.

3. GLENN AND I TOOK A TRIP TO NEW ORLEANS with my sister and her husband, Dan, for our fifth anniversary, their tenth. New Orleans was once, will be again, the ultimate destination for authentic American cuisine. Accordingly, Glenn and I planned to eat our way across town, gumbo to beignet, from sunup to sundown. I was six months pregnant with Lucy and in free-for-all eating mode. Add to that the indulge-yourself vacation vibe, plus the ninety-degree heat that made it nearly impossible to do anything *but* go to restaurants.

The highlight of that trip was dinner at Emeril's flagship restaurant in the French Quarter. Emeril Lagasse was, at the time, the most famous chef in America. I couldn't believe our luck, getting a reservation only a few weeks in advance. How I anticipated this meal! I'd sink into a cream-and-cayenne trance, daydreaming about it. The food itself definitely lived

up to the hype. Course after course of revelatory flavor, unlike anything in New York. We each ordered an appetizer,
entrée, and dessert and passed our plates around the table so
we could sample everything. Two memorable dishes blew
my socks off. The oyster stew was so flavorful and spicy, every spoonful was an explosion on the tongue. Also, at that
meal, I had my very first chocolate soufflé. We'd had to pre-
order because the dessert took an hour to prepare. When the
waiter brought it to our table, he poured hot chocolate sauce
into its pillowed heart. Dazzled the senses. I nearly cried
when I had my first bite.

The wine flowed like water. So did the conversation. Although Alison and I had mutual friends in college (she was
two years ahead of me at Dartmouth), we weren't friends
ourselves, per se. Yes, yes, we love each other, best friends for
life and all that, but the two of us were just too different
growing up to be buddies. Let me put it this way: Alison was
a straitlaced, straight-A type. She was a selective dater,
drug-averse, an upstanding citizen. We all know what I was.
Alison deplored many of my adventurous life choices over
the years. In high school, she ratted me out about cigarettes
in my purse, a stash box under the bed, a six-pack of Meisterbräu in the bushes. I'd been with scores of men in half a
dozen countries. Alison had had only one serious boyfriend.
And, reader, she married him! Archetypically, we fit the
models of responsible, superachiever firstborn and rebellious,
free-spirit secondborn. We had little in common, except for
growing up in the same house, going to the same college,
and having issues with Mom. Place meant nothing, though.
We might as well have been living on different planets, given

the widely disparate experiences we had at home and school.

Despite our day/night personalities, somehow Alison and I had wound up in the same stage of life. Since I'd gotten married and had Maggie (and was about to have Lucy), Alison and I had more to talk about. She and Dan had two daughters. We were both journalists and worked at magazines. During that meal, I felt like Alison and I had a "friend" breakthrough. She wasn't my protective, disapproving older sister at Emeril's. At thirty-three and thirty-four, we were finally about to relate to each other as peers, pals who'd chosen to travel together. Seeing Alison as an equal that night was a giant step forward in terms of how I saw myself. I was a fully fledged person now. A mother and wife, a responsible, upstanding citizen, just like her. My druggie slutty life was behind me, and that meal closed the door on it.

4. I WAS THIRTY-EIGHT, AND MADLY IN LOVE. Glenn had died two and a half years before, in November 2000. Ten months later, in August 2001, I met Steve and, in short order, fell in love again. In the spring of 2003, we were still in the infatuation period, thrilling at each other's slightest touch. We took every opportunity to indulge ourselves in each other, and that often included food. One early afternoon, I received the news that one of my novels had been optioned by a famous actress to be the source material for a Hollywood movie. Steve and I made the spontaneous decision to celebrate over lunch at the Oyster Bar in Grand Central Station in Manhattan. The kids were at school until three. Considering travel time, we would have one hour to eat.

We sat at the raw bar, reserved for diners who wanted their lunch served on the half shell on a bed of ice. Steve and I started by ordering two dozen oysters, as well as beers. We were in our own world, sliding the pliant glistening meat onto our tongues, staring into each other's eyes, licking lips, etc. If I were a crotchety prude seated nearby and had to watch a thirty-eight-year-old woman and a forty-nine-year-old man feeding each other oysters in a frankly sexual manner, I'd have thrown down my tiny fork and stormed out of there disgusted. We continued to be disgusting for another dozen oysters, another round of beer. Then we took the train back to Brooklyn to pick up the kids at school.

That lunch—escaping into the city to delight our senses, to visit our private universe of two, and then contentedly return to reality—was emblematic of the thrill of Steve, of the salty sea change he'd brought. My existence as a widowed mother had been lonely, sad, bleak, joyless. Steve rode in and turned my life into a fun, passionate adventure—during off-parenting hours. On-parenting hours, he was great with the kids, making them fall in love with him, too. Steve made me happy again. The movie option? It was a fantastic validation of my work, but an emotional blip compared to the incomparable joy and relief that my heart hadn't stopped beating when Glenn's had. My life with Steve was only just beginning.

5. A YEAR LATER, STEVE AND I GOT MARRIED. We threw a clambake at my parents' farmhouse in Thetford, Vermont. The ceremony itself was lovely. Steve and my dad played a duet of "Aura Lee" (aka "Love Me Tender") on their French horns. Our siblings and friends made funny and tear-jerking

speeches for us. The girls and I wore white. We stood together, as if Steve were marrying all three of us.

Indeed, Maggie had been responsible for our setting the date for the wedding. We'd been quasi-engaged for a while already, and then one morning, Maggie asked Steve, "When are you going to buy Mom the engagement ring you promised her?" Hand to God, I did not put her up to it. The four of us went to a jewelry store that afternoon after school.

Steve had said before that, had it not been for the girls, we probably never would have married. Both of us being middle-aged, we'd decided not to have children together. We had separate finances, and planned to keep it that way. There hadn't been any real reason to marry, except the girls wanted to make it legal. Maggie, eight at the time, was firm on this point. It wasn't enough that her mom had a boyfriend. She didn't want a stepboyfriend. She wanted a step*father*. Truth be told, I wasn't satisfied with "boyfriend," either. I wanted "husband."

Second weddings are traditionally small. Ours was only sixty people. The vows exchanged, the license signed, the sun came out from behind a cloud (true), and the festivities continued with a spread of honest food. Lobsters, barbecued chicken and ribs, baked potatoes, corn on the cob, biscuits. We'd spent a lot of time in Maine with Steve's family by then, and my daughters had cracked quite a few claws. At the wedding, Maggie, nine, and Lucy, six, tucked into lobster after lobster like seasoned pros. Maggie must have eaten four whole lobsters that day. Lucy drank straight from the little cups of melted butter. At one point, she accidentally spilled some on her white dress. My parents' golden retriever, Jake, volunteered to help her clean up. One of my favorite wedding pictures is of Lucy standing with her arms at her sides, looking down at Jake licking the golden stain on her dress, his tail a blur. Talk about the joy of real butter; we can learn a lot from our animal friends. Both girls flitted from guest to guest, acting as hostesses, reveling in the attention. Lucy made a speech about how her first father died and, as sad as that had been, now we had Steve, who made us a whole family again. Let me tell you, when a six-year-old grabs the microphone and talks philosophically about death and rebirth, you won't find a dry eye in the house.

As much as that day was about Steve and me, it was about the girls. Despite the hardship they'd already faced in their young lives, they were happy, healthy, socially adept, insightful, wonderful kids. They hadn't been damaged permanently, as I'd feared. On the contrary. They'd rallied, recovered, and recognized our incredible luck when we saw it in Steve.

Looking over this list of meals and memories, it seemed obvious that positive thoughts about food were connected to love and success. Positive thoughts about *life* were connected to love and success. If A equaled C, and B equaled C, then A and B had to be the same.

Food was life.

And all along, I thought food was the Grim Reaper.

Nancy was right. Real ingredients won't kill me. On the contrary, real butter, and real happiness, will only make me stronger.

I called her. "Butter is my friend," I announced. I filled her in on my thought process.

"So you'll throw out the Smart Balance and Splenda?" Nancy asked.

I wasn't willing to go *that* far. "When I cook and bake, I'll use the real thing. With coffee, a little Splenda won't kill me, either."

"Moderation," she said. "A novel concept. Sounds reasonable."

Indeed, as the weeks ticked by, "reasonable" was overriding "irrational" as the mental operating system of choice.

9

THE ALL-CONSUMING STORY OF STEVE

Steve and I began our love affair as disembodied entities, fantasies constructed in part by imagination, and fleshed out with hopes, dreams, biographical details, and the mysterious spaces between typed words. In other words, we met online.

I'd started visiting dating sites after about six months of single motherhood. I was curious about what was out there. I needed to feel hope. I agreed with my family and friends that I wasn't quite "ready" for a serious relationship. But I was definitely ready—*beyond* ready—to have sex. My friend Judith told me early on in my widowhood that she'd read it was common for the grieving spouse to use sex as a life-affirming act, an antidote to the ill effects of months mired in disease. I was desperate for some relief from my grief, and I decided sex was just the ticket. It'd been a reliable distraction—if temporary—in the past. I found myself fantasizing wildly about a few men I knew. When I wasn't dealing with reality—cooking, cleaning, schlepping, digging out from under the avalanche of death-related paperwork—I would lie on my bed and watch XXX-rated movies of the mind, all starring me (thinner) and a fantasy lover.

Fantasy might have been a subconscious protective buffer. I could have used those hours to think about my lonely life and replay horrible scenes from the year before. I decided my brain knew what it was doing. I let it go into the nooks, crannies, and orifices it wanted to go into.

In terms of real sex, I halfheartedly tried to seduce a cute single colleague of Glenn's. I'd always thought he was sexy. This man was responsive to my flirty e-mails at first, but when I suggested we meet for lunch, he freaked out and stopped answering my messages. Poor bastard. I can only imagine how I seemed to him, a desperate, horny widow. Well, I was! I'm not ashamed to admit the truth. I defy anyone who hasn't been a thirty-five-year-old widow to judge. It'd been quite a while since I'd had sex. My weight was at a seven-year low. Although my husband was dead, my libido was very much alive.

I told a friend that when I got back into action, I would screw a different guy every month for a year. After that time, depending on how I liked the variety, I'd either keep going or look for a man with relationship potential.

With that goal in mind, I went on several dates—one fix-up, mostly guys I met online. I could barely stand to have lunch with them, let alone give them blowjobs. I had an almost erotic encounter with (this is so pathetically predictable) a trainer at my gym. He came over to give me a free massage. Afterward, we shared a joint. He was young and sexy. I was stoned and naked under a towel. It was one of the least erotic evenings of my life. I felt nothing. Not the slightest twinge. He was as shocked as I was when I said I had an early morning. He folded his massage table, grabbed his bag of oils, and left. Through neighborhood gossip, I heard that he'd hooked up with another single-mother gym-goer and wound up having an exclusive relationship with her that lasted over a year.

Undeterred by my conflicting impulses (lurid fantasy life, frigid social life), I pressed on with the online search for a lover. I came across Steve's profile, the title of which was "This Ad Is Not Stupid!" Funny. I read his entry and laughed a couple of times at his witty remarks. I sent him an e-mail. He sent one back. We continued to exchange notes and pictures for two months before actually meeting (logistical difficulties; we took turns being out of town or unavailable). Our first date was in August 2001, at a dive bar on Lispenard Street, which, a month later, was deep in the red zone.

With the exception of our e-mailing and first three dates, our entire relationship has been post-9/11. I wonder if that's been relevant, in terms of our instant, intense attachment. You hear a lot about the glut of post-9/11 babies. Sex *is* life-affirming in the wake of tragedy. Maybe I needed double the life-affirmation. And Steve was the man for the job. From our second date on, Steve and I behaved like fornicating bunnies. When the kids were at my in-laws' for the weekend, Steve and I would have forty-eight-hour fuck fests; we'd get out of bed only to use the bathroom or eat sexy food (think succulent, juicy, firm).

I was a size ten. If not thin, I was in great shape, running three or four times a week. I assumed Steve was the kind of guy who loved ample women. He complimented me constantly and made me feel beautiful, irresistible. Everyone could see how happy I was, including the girls. I'd kept them in the loop, told them that I was seeing someone, a musician/opera singer/actor, and that we had afternoon dates when they were at school. I showed them Steve's headshot at his opera company's Web site. Eventually, Steve came over for dinner to meet Maggie and Lucy, then six and three. Shortly after that, I took the girls—and my parents, and Alison and her family—to Carnegie Hall to see Steve star as Ko-Ko in a production of *The Mikado*. When he took his bows onstage, he squinted to locate us in our front row seats and waved at Maggie and Lucy. Steve started sleeping over at our apartment. We introduced each other to our friends. Our sex turned into more-than-sex. I already knew that my plan of sleeping with a guy a month for a year was not going to happen. I laughed with my friends about how the first guy I slept with after Glenn might be the last guy I have sex with ever again. Around our six-month anniversary, Steve and I talked about getting married. We were lazily stroking each other, in a state of physical and emotional bliss.

"I adore every inch of your body," he said. "And it'd be even better if you could get rid of the stomach."

Sound of a needle scratching across a record. That was what I heard in my head when he brought up my bane, my stomach flab. For six months, he'd made me feel like the most beautiful woman alive. I'd had a six-month period of not worrying or caring about my body flaws—because of the way he'd treated me. The subconscious shelf I'd put my bad body image up on came crashing down. All my old fat fears were now scattered across the bed between us. In a rush, I mentally scanned the photos he'd shown me of his ex-girlfriends, dancers and actresses, all of them slim. I was instantly convinced he'd lied about every nice thing he'd ever said to me, that he'd been faking his passion for me. Covering myself, I was too shocked to speak, cry, or defend myself. I was naked, in every way you can be naked.

When I told friends, they were horrified. Rebecca said, "He wants you to lose weight? Tell him to grow a few inches."

In the following weeks, I strived to take his request at face value. Hadn't he proved he loved me and desired me a hundred times over? If I'd had a complaint about his body, didn't I have a right to mention it to him? He hadn't meant to insult me. He didn't know about my complicated issues with body image. One of the things I'd loved most about our relationship was the here-and-now-ness of it. We'd dutifully talked about our childhood (pets, camps, siblings) and old relationships, but we'd skipped deep discussion about our emotional histories of angst, insecurity, and (in his case) depression. I'd wanted to reinvent myself for Steve, and I was not going to dust off the ancient stories about how mean Mom used to be or what a loser I was in junior high. I remembered telling my friends what a relief it'd been, not having to dredge up the past. The mature woman Steve knew was strong, sexy, and secure. Little did he know that when it came to fat, I was a whimpering, quivering infant.

Remembering that night, I can smell my own fear of losing him. No matter how hard you try to ignore your issues, they will creep out of dark corners when goaded by the slightest provocation.

I kicked into "on" diet mode, like the veteran I was. Steve had never seen me on a full-scale diet. He was impressed by my perfectionism, the intensity of my commitment. He thought I was doing it for him. I thought I was, too, and I was motivated by wanting to please him. I started running longer distances, eventually working up to a half marathon of thirteen miles (a feat I have yet to repeat). I stopped eating carbs *completely* (not a mild Zone but full-blown Atkins). After several months of pure perfection, at the age of thirty-seven, I was back to my twenty-three-year-old weight. Size eight jeans were roomy on me. I could fit into the size six backless dress I wore the night I met Glenn. I tried on the dress one night for Steve, amazed I could get into it. I twirled for him. He applauded. I was showing (myself) off, and he was duly appreciative. As well he should've been.

Predictably, the compliments came rolling in. Losing weight—this time, about twenty pounds—was a magnet for public commentary. At school drop-off, mothers said, "You've melted!" and "How'd you get so skinny?" At one of the interminable parent potluck dinners, a father I barely knew came up to me and said, "Wow, you've lost a ton of weight." He turned to his wife. "Doesn't she look great?" His wife was not so impressed. Nor was I by the left-handed compliment. I smiled contemptuously at the idiot husband, and apologetically at the jealous wife. Still, I did walk away with a lightness in my step.

As if I were in a tunnel, I heard the echoes from my sixth-grade teacher and the mothers of Short Hills. The rush of public acclaim for having made less of myself felt exactly the same at thirty-eight as it had at eleven. I was a mother myself now, and as hungry for approval as the needy child I used to be. I'd survived high school, gone to college, seduced scores of men, written a dozen books, made money, bought an apartment, married, had kids, been widowed, but I hadn't really changed at all. Not about this.

And what of Steve? Did my half-marathoner body make him love me more? Make love to me with deeper ardor? Were his kisses extratender, or his whispers sweeter? Not at all. He said he enjoyed my pride in myself. On an aesthetic level, he liked the slimmer silhouette. But he withheld the ultimate reward, what I longed to hear: that he knew I'd scraped and sacrificed *for him,* and he appreciated my hard work. It's sick, I realize, but I desperately wanted him to be pleased that he'd made me suffer.

I owned up to none of these thoughts and feelings. Instead, I pranced around in a lot of lingerie and/or sweaty running shorts and waited for something about our relationship to change as dramatically as my waistline. I might as well have been waiting for the second coming of Christ. By my lights, Steve and I were stalled. I'd done my part. So where was the rush of . . . actually, I don't know *what* big change I was expecting. He continued to ravish me nightly. He professed his love as before. Our home life followed the usual routine. Our professional lives proceeded apace. That was the problem. Steve acted as if nothing important had changed.

My frustration with him was a major cause, but it was inevitable that I'd relax my standards. I started to skip runs on the flimsiest excuse. I became reacquainted with breadstuffs.

I cycled into a new (but, really, so very old) dieting pattern of off-and-on. Whenever Steve went on tour with his opera company, I'd diet frantically, hoping to wow him with a hot bod upon his return. That plan was inherently flawed. Lonely nights were my undoing. When he came home, I'd prepare elaborate meals for us to linger over. I'd blow off the gym to loll in bed with him in the mornings, then simmer all afternoon in silent guilt. Resentment surfaced. Often, I'd willfully eat the kids' junk food in his presence, practically daring him to say something.

In three months, I'd re-gained the twenty pounds I'd lost. Dieter's whiplash. One day I was thin. The next day, my new size-eight wardrobe was suffocatingly tight. Along the way, I complained about the rapid re-gain with Alison. "It's Mom all over again," she said. "You're rebelling."

I didn't completely agree. Mom had tormented me daily. Steve had said, just once, that he'd like to see me without the belly. I had reason to be hurt by Steve's request, but no reason to be spiteful.

"I don't mean you're rebelling against Steve," said Alison. "You're still rebelling against Mom."

Okay, that rang true. Unwittingly, Steve churned up the old toxic dust. He didn't deserve to be punished for his simple request, one that any spouse, male or female, had the right to make. Steve had been only loving to me. He cleaned my apartment, did my laundry, kept me company, made love to me. He'd taken on a widow with two small kids, and saved us all. If he asked me (on gentle wings) to tighten my gut, so what? If that was the worst he could dish out, I should be grateful.

Instead, I'd tried to win his approval by losing weight, just as I had in elementary school with Mom. Then I rebelled against his wishes, just as I had in high school with Mom. Throw in a little "gain weight to test the love" action, as I'd done with Glenn. Would I gain a full forty pounds to test Steve's love?

I asked myself, "Does anything about this have to do with Steve?" It took the better part of a year to get from the night of the belly comment to facing the real issues of our relationship. Yes, Steve had brought joy back into our lives. He was a heck of a lot of fun, a positive influence for the kids. But. Steve was a middle-aged never-married actor who traveled a lot. Would he be the father the girls deserved? Could I be sure he was truly committed to such a huge responsibility? It was entirely possible, once our infatuation wore off, he'd think twice about the life I offered him. Just how devastating would it be for Maggie and Lucy if Steve decided to leave?

I'd spent five months obsessed with an all-consuming diet, and the following three months depressed about falling off the Atkins wagon. Twenty pounds were lost and re-gained. I'd made no progress answering the important questions about our relationship. It was the same old drill, running to stand still.

You know what happened. Maggie pressed the point, demanded that we set a wedding date. Steve and I planned the ceremony and party as a team, which gave me confidence about his commitment. We got married and made everyone cry. I wore a size-ten Nicole Miller dress, sleeveless (although I was anxious about my arms). *The New York Times* covered the wedding for the Sunday Styles section Vows column, and it was exciting to see our photo in the paper and to read the accompanying article. The piece was sweet, sentimental. The reporter hit the right notes. Of course, she didn't mention the parallel story of my weight and how it moved up and down as our relationship evolved.

We'd been married for three years. Our sex life was still wonderful, but it wasn't what it used to be. We'd sometimes go a week without doing it. My friends assured me that this was hardly a cause for concern. But if Steve didn't roll toward me when the lights went out, my immediate thought was "He doesn't want me. He thinks I'm fat." That stomach comment just wouldn't die in my mind. Apparently, some negative thoughts weren't easily controlled. To vanquish it, I'd have to talk to Steve about it. Which I planned to do.

But first, I had a bigger item on the agenda.

10

THE MOTHER LOAD, PART TWO

The Frankels were a family of talkers. Steve thought we were a family of yellers (his family is practically mute by comparison). We scrapped for the last word, used volume like a tool. We repeated, rehashed, diced, and sliced language down to the syllable—was it any wonder Alison and I were both writers? We could talk until blue-faced about nearly any subject, be it politics, movies, books, gossip, philosophy, gardening. When we watched a movie or TV show together, non-Frankels tore their hair out because we talked incessantly over it. Steve refused to watch movies with my family. Can't say I blame him.

I'd probably exchanged more words with my mother than with any other person on earth, many of them swapped at the kitchen table, newspapers strewn around coffee mugs. For all our yakking, however, Mom and I avoided certain subjects, running an obstacle course of conversation to do so. My teenage years. Her obsessive fatphobia. My current weight.

"Why bother bringing it up?" I said to myself. "Judy and I are fine now." There was no point in dragging our skeletons into the light.

Until now. Dragging skeletons into the light had become my day job.

I'd been channeling a lot of old anger into sweaty sessions on the treadmill for six months since I began emotional housecleaning. I'd lost weight, firmed up. A neighborhood friend noticed the change and asked me what my goals were. Ten pounds, fifteen? I shook my head. "My goals are emotional," I said. I hadn't weighed myself since the summer. I hadn't been dieting. No carb was off-limits. The world of food was a cornucopia of availability. I'd eat when hungry, stop when full, sample to satisfy a craving, but I hadn't pigged out on sweets or chips, evidentiary proof that I wanted only what I told myself I shouldn't have.

The Not Diet was working. I was on an even keel with food and exercise. My skips down memory lane had been helping, too. Emotional excavation was painful while it was happening, but a relief afterward. Nonetheless, as the holidays approached, a laziness came over me, like a warm comforter that made it hard to get out of bed. I started to slack off, skipping the gym, waving the banner of not-dieting too often and eating past the point of full for the sake of it. I felt the coming of a low-grade depression, a malaise. I slogged through the last-minute holiday shopping and travel planning. We were going first to Maine to Steve's family and then to Vermont to my parents' farmhouse. I was grouchy about spending hours in the car, the abundance of family, the kids on a nonstop sugar train, the pressure of gift giving. My mood was dark.

What better time for a decades-delayed emotional confrontation?

A few days after Christmas, I got my chance. Alison and her family had left Vermont to return to Long Island. We were leaving for Brooklyn the next day. The kids and Steve were playing outside in the snow. My parents and I were at the kitchen table (where else?) with the newspaper and coffee.

Mom was talking about her volunteer work at pediatric hospitals with her golden retrievers. One cancer kid asked her why she loved dogs so much. "I explained to him that when I was a little girl I was left alone a lot, and my best friend was my German shepherd, Duchess," she said. Mom went on about how Duchess was her confidante. Duchess adored her. When her family ignored her or made her feel worthless, she had her dog to love.

I said, "Did you then tell the cancer kid that when you grew up and had a daughter of your own, you, in turn, made her feel worthless?"

Whoosh. Every window in the house was closed tight, but we all felt the malevolent wind blow through.

Mom braced against the table. "Okay," she said. "We're going to do this now? Let's go." Judy knew I was writing a memoir about body image. I'd already interviewed her about Fay, her mother. She must've suspected this confrontation was coming.

I pointed at a recent photo of Lucy taped to the refrigerator. "Look at her," I said. "That's how old I was when you started in on me. If I snatched a cookie out of Lucy's hand, said she was too fat and wasn't allowed to have cookies again, she'd be crushed. The only thing she'd understand was that I was angry, that she'd done something terrible."

"You ate twice as much as Alison and Jon," said Mom. "You were always asking for food. When you were eight, our pediatrician told us we were going to have to keep a close eye on your weight."

"Did the pediatrician tell you to humiliate me, and yell at me, and punish me for eating? Did he tell you to cry and scream if I ate too much?"

"You were incredibly frustrating," said Mom. "I tried to control you, but you kept eating."

"Did it occur to you that making threats wasn't the best strategy?"

"If I didn't yell, you'd eat *more,*" she said. "I'd get more frustrated, and I'd yell more. It's not like I was the only mother who did it. We all did it." She rattled off a few names, moms from New Jersey I'd known my whole life. Among their daughters, I counted an anorexic, a bulimic, a binge eater, and a morbidly obese woman. "We talked about it a lot," said Mom. "We all felt the same way. We didn't want overweight kids."

"So you were all fatphobic," I said. "That doesn't make it right."

Howie jumped in. "We were concerned that you'd grow up to be obese."

"Why would you think that?" I asked. "You're a doctor. You had to know that obesity is mainly genetic. We don't have obesity on either side of the family."

"Look at it from our perspective," he said. "We had three kids. Two of them were skinny, one of them tended to be chubby. We didn't want you to get fat, so we tried to control you. In retrospect, it worked out okay. We kept at you, and your weight stayed in a reasonable range."

"But that wasn't the only thing that mattered. What about my sense of security?" I asked. "You can't believe shrieking at a little kid about every bite of food is good for her."

He said, "I don't remember that."

Why would he? He was a young doctor, working sixty and seventy hours per week. When he was home, late at night and on some weekends, Judy reined it in. She tended to be most explosive when overwhelmed by the demands of daily life. Those demands were lessened when Dad was home to help.

"Just admit that it wasn't about health or fear for my future obesity," I said. "You didn't want a fat kid because she'd be a bad reflection on you."

Dad said, "A lot of time has gone by. I just don't remember. Your weight was just one small part of my life back then."

True. But for Mom, alas, my weight was her number-one concern. I said to her, "I know you remember, Judy. The relentlessness."

"Relentlessness is a part of my personality," she said. "And I admit one hundred percent that it was about aesthetics for me. I was not concerned about your health. I wanted you to be slim because I don't like fat. That's just who I am. It's cultural, part of my own family history growing up. My mother was relentless about my brother's weight. Until the day she died, she was on him about it."

"If you hated her so much, why were you just like her?" I asked.

"When I got frustrated, I couldn't control myself," said

Judy. "You can hate something about the way you were raised and still wind up repeating the mistakes. Yes, I yelled. I screamed. I was not going to give up, and I never got tired of trying to get you to lose weight. I understand you have issues about it and that things are handled differently now. But I did what I felt I had to do."

I knew Judy would never apologize. When I tried therapy in my early twenties, my shrink said these magical words to me: "Your mother is not going to change. You can either fight her to the death, or accept her for who she is and just deal with it." That sentiment was one of my main excuses for not confronting Judy. And now, I was wondering if I should have bothered. What satisfaction was there to be gained, if she refused to admit she'd been wrong?

"Why do you refuse to say it was wrong to terrorize an eleven-year-old?" I asked.

"It wasn't ideal," she said. "But if I could go back, I don't think I'd act differently."

"You made yourself my enemy. You turned my weight into a battle of wills," I said. "It felt like you were trying to break me. To squash my spirit."

"I just wanted you to lose ten pounds!" said Judy. "If you'd've done what I wanted, we wouldn't be having this conversation."

A lifetime of baggage over ten fucking pounds.

"Your love felt conditional," I said. "I questioned whether you cared about me. Whether you even liked me, unless I was thin."

"I wanted you to be thin—I fought for it—*because* I loved you," she said.

I'd run out of questions. I wouldn't get the answers I wanted anyway. I got up from the table, packed the kids and duffels into the car, and we left for Brooklyn within the hour. Dad called the next day and said Mom was upset. She cried all night about how I'd accused her of being a bad mother. I told him that I refused to apologize to her, that she should apologize to me. I had every right to be angry. He said solemnly, "I want you to apologize anyway."

What could I do? I called back in an hour and apologized.

11

THE NAKED TRUTH

"want to pose nude," I told Paula, my editor at *Self* magazine.

We were at lunch. I told her about my vow to rid myself of my fat obsession. I explained that I'd been striving to lay myself bare, strip away the past, cast my body image in a new light. I'd been so focused on the problem areas, I said, I'd lost sight of the big picture. Now, I wanted to see it—see myself, for exactly what I was. The only way to confront reality was to pose naked. Artsy nude. Not beaver shots or flying boobs. Think tasteful, flirty. I had the name of a photographer, Koren Reyes, who specialized in nude portraits of women over forty. I'd do the shoot, then write about the experience in an essay for *Self*.

Paula loved the idea. But . . . "We can't publish the article without running the pictures, too."

I was afraid she'd say that. Hesitantly, I nodded.

Before calling the photographer, I had to psych myself up for months. When I finally made contact, Koren described her philosophy. "Women over forty don't get as much appreciation as they should," she said. "Women of all ages, shapes, and sizes are beautiful."

Yes, well, *of course*. "Have you ever photographed an exceedingly large woman?" I asked.

"I worked with someone who weighed well over two hundred pounds. The pictures turned out great," she said.

That was reassuring. If she could make a plus-size woman look good, perhaps she could make me look like Heidi Klum. "I'm seeing this experience as a final step down the long, long—*really* long—road to self-acceptance," I said.

Koren refused to promise everlasting serenity or to vanquish my demons. She was willing to say this, however: "Everyone I've worked with has had a positive experience." I almost asked for that in writing. We set a date for six weeks hence.

The upcoming shoot loomed on the surface of my consciousness, if abstractly. When I told people of my plans, they thought I was "crazy" or "brave," which I took to be mildly insulting. Nancy made me laugh myself sick one night, demonstrating (dressed) potential poses such as "the Frog," "Rex at the Hydrant," and "Dropped the Soap." The future shoot was a punch line, a lark. And seemingly far, far away. Until it was suddenly right upon me.

A week prior, Koren sent a confirmation e-mail. She'd rented a space, hired a makeup artist and an assistant. I gulped hard when I read the e-mail. The shoot *wasn't* abstract or a lark. It was real and serious—and too late to back out. I was horrified that other people would be there, watching.

I did my level best to make myself presentable on the day

before the shoot. I depilated my legs, arms, belly, chin, lip, eyebrows, and armpits. Should the photos ever be examined under a microscope, not a single unwanted hair would be found. Going for a natural look, I removed toe and fingernail polish. I exfoliated and moisturized. Twice.

Smooth and pink, I arrived at the studio on time, at nine in the morning. I'd skipped breakfast, hoping that would make me appear ten pounds slimmer. Maggie, the assistant, a photographer herself with many artist friends, told me she'd posed nude countless times. "Full body, topless, alone or in groups," she said as if it were nothing. I figured if Maggie, curvy and redheaded, could do it, so could I.

Yuko, the rail-thin hair and makeup artist, was soft-spoken and sweet. She intended to do wonders with my head. Of course, that would still leave a significant amount of flesh unattended.

Koren arrived a few minutes later. Trim and stylish, she gave the immediate impression of professional competence. We talked about poses. I tried to seem cool and comfortable, but inside, I was churning.

When Yuko was done with me, I dashed into the bathroom, stripped, and put on a bathrobe. I returned to the studio, a cavernous space with umbrella lights. A roll of white paper—a "seamless"—was pulled down one wall and across the floor. I started to sweat even though the room was cold. Koren, camera in hand, directed me onto the seamless. Maggie tested the lighting. Then Koren said, "Lose the robe."

This was virgin territory. I had been nude in the presence of women only in fitting and locker rooms. I love locker rooms for showcasing the incredible diversity of the female form. But one didn't linger there. I'd never been fully, flagrantly naked for longer than five minutes in sight of other females. Now, I would be starkers in front of three, for hours.

I took a deep breath, paused, and shrugged off my robe. I wasn't expecting applause, but something other than dead silence would've been nice. When I disrobed for men—especially for the first time—they always said *something* complimentary, even if out of sheer politeness. These women, on the other hand, stared quietly at my nudity. Not stared at—*studied*. They examined me like a specimen, seeing what they had to work with. I nearly said, "Hello! Naked person here! A kind word needed!"

I remembered the *Brady Bunch* adage, "When you're nervous, imagine the audience in their underwear." Perhaps not the best idea, given the situation. Instead, I imagined *myself* in my underwear.

Koren said, "Okay, sit down facing me, cross your legs at the ankle, and fold your arms over your knees."

And, just like my clothes, we were off. While I arranged myself into position, I twisted mentally, too. The lack of flattery bothered me. Then again, convincing me of my attractiveness was not Koren's job. That was *my* job, one I'd failed at chronically.

Concentrating on Koren's directions ("drop the shoulders," "chin down") helped me forget the terror. Yuko and Maggie watched from behind her. Smiley Yuko nodded encouragingly and said, "Beautiful!" over and over again, which I dearly appreciated. Maggie's technical, terse "good" and "nice" commentary also soothed. When I started to loosen up, Koren asked more of me. "You're a *Playboy* model!" she said. "Act like you're caught coming out of the shower!" And "Pout for me." I must have looked like a deranged porn star, because Koren said, "Not like that! On second thought, don't pout. Ever." That made me laugh hard and resulted in, I later saw, some of the day's brightest smiles.

Since we were all working toward the common goal—pretty pictures—nudity started to feel productive and purposeful (as opposed to exposed and vulnerable). The awkwardness of being undressed with women also diminished. Unlike my usual frame of reference, this nudity was decidedly nonsexual. I was reminded of the one time, on Martha's Vineyard, I went to a nude beach and nakedness was free, natural—fun.

I posed sitting, standing, kneeling, lying on my belly and back. Modeling was hard work. Poses that might appear natural were anything but. As I struggled to do what Koren asked, I occasionally paused to think, "I can't believe I'm flat on my back with my tits hanging out *in public*."

Koren seemed pleased by what she was getting. And, as the day progressed, I became convinced pulchritude was possible. For one pose, Yuko arranged my hair to curl over my shoulder. When I rested my cheek on my knee, strands swept across my back. It felt good; I smiled dreamily. Maggie said an emphatic "Nice!" and I had a veritable "I Feel Pretty" moment. I compared that to my habitual self-annihilation in the mirror, how I zeroed in on the ugly. Artists searched for beauty. I made a vow to look at myself with an artistic sensibility.

The shoot lasted all morning. We ran out of ideas right when lunch arrived. Relieved it was over, I practically inhaled my sandwich. Koren asked what I thought of the experience. I admitted that I'd been tense at first. "But after ten minutes," I said, "I saw the humor of it. How could rolling around on the floor in the buff be anything but comic?"

It could be tragic, if the pictures were awful. Koren showed me some of the images in the tiny box on her digital camera. The size of a postage stamp, they didn't look hideous. She promised to e-mail me the lot tomorrow.

Seeing the portfolio the next day was a revelation. Granted, my belly looked like a deflated beach ball in some shots. Lying on my side squashed my boobs into pancakes. But most of the pictures were quite presentable. In about half of them, I looked downright cute. In a dozen, I would call myself hot. Not thin, of course—but, as I was beginning to understand, thin wasn't necessarily equal to good. Good wasn't necessarily equal to thin. The range of thin was itself narrow. The universe of good was vast and ever expanding.

Steve loved the pictures. "Most nude models look pissed off or mean," he said. "Your pictures are sexy in a completely nonthreatening way. You look like you had a good time." I realized I had. A great time.

I pored over the portfolio for days, hardly flinching at the deflated-beach-ball and pancake-breast shots. I discounted them as bad angles. With so many better angles to choose from, the bad ones hardly mattered.

I was learning to edit, both my photo portfolio and my critical thoughts. My husband suggested we frame some prints, for the posterity of my posterior. I reserved a spot on the shelf next to my bedroom mirror and decided to use the print as rebuttal evidence against the harsh inner monologist, should she speak up again.

Which, actually, she hadn't. Since the shoot, the critical chatter had been barely audible. Apparently, the more you showed of yourself, the less you cared. The photos had turned me away from the negative and toward the positive. Instead of fixating on my flabby gut, my eyes started to go to my strong legs, soft shoulders, pretty face. The photos had shown me what was right before my eyes all along. Beauty had been hiding in plain sight. Now I could see it.

Even my mom agreed that I looked good (in some shots).

I had to wait a few months before the article and photos were published in *Self* (February 2007, check 'em out!). A few days before the issue hit the newsstands, a copy arrived in my mailbox. Steve and I picked up the package on the way out to dinner. We opened the magazine and quickly found the right page. Not one, not two, not three, but *six photos* of naked me accompanied my essay. My stomach flopped. I'd seen the pictures. I'd examined them dozens of times in the last months to reassure myself that I wasn't completely nutso whacko cuckoo to allow them to be published. I could practically draw each image from memory. As I suddenly realized, though, it was one thing to pose for photos, another to look at them in the privacy of my home, and quite another to see them published in a major national magazine with a readership of five million people.

I almost puked, right into the open magazine in the vestibule of our building. Steve said, "Wow. Six pictures. That's ballsy, Val."

He had to hold my elbow as we walked outside. The cold air made me feel less queasy. We went to an Indian restaurant on Montague Street. Steve had the magazine open to my story while we ordered. I watched the waiter glance at the pictures, turn to me to take my order, do a double take, and then blush furiously before he hurried away to get our Taj Mahals.

That made us laugh, and I relaxed. Each time the waiter came to our table, he stammered and fumbled. I started to feel sorry for the guy. Poor bastard was picturing me naked while dishing out the curry. As awkward as it was for him, I liked his nervousness. If I'd known the power appearing nude would give me over men, I'd have done this a lot sooner.

I could tell which of the moms at my daughters' school were *Self* readers by the way they stared at me at pickup. One mother blushed and giggled whenever she saw me. Others congratulated me on my guts (never seen in such a favorable light before), on how lovely I looked (what else could they say?), and on the article itself. The reactions from complete strangers were more satisfying. Dozens of e-mails came in via my Web site, praising my courage and conviction. Several readers made plans to get their own naked photos taken, and I encouraged and thanked them all in reply e-mails that might have been embarrassingly gushy ("Thank you so, so much for writing. You don't know what this means to me. I'm really beyond grateful . . ."). The letters flooded into *Self* also. None were negative, as in, "What, you're photographing walruses now?"

When Lucy saw the piece, she hugged me and told me how proud she was. I felt like a positive role model, an example for her to follow (not by posing nude in a magazine, goes without saying, certainly not until she's forty-one). One day, she had her friend Maria over, and I found the two of them with their heads together, poring over the article and photos. My instinct was to snatch it away, but I resisted. Nudity wasn't shameful. My photos weren't obscene. The whole point was to take pride in myself—Lucy must have been proud of me to show it to her friend—and that was a good message for all women, eight to eighty. Maria looked up from the magazine and said simply, "You look great." No apparent trauma. Her voice was normal. Her mother wouldn't call me later to accuse me of scarring her daughter for life. I thanked Maria, and they went off to play.

Maggie, on the other hand, hated the piece. Of course, she was eleven, on the cusp of her big transformation. She found anything nudity-related to be deathly embarrassing. My parents sent an e-mail applauding the "tastefulness" of the shots. My sister said the story was "well done." (I thought it was "raw.") My friend Judith told me that her online community chat room had been hotly discussing the piece and photos. The point of debate? Whether or not the photos were retouched, and therefore defeating the purpose of laying myself bare. What made them suspicious of Photoshopping? The absence of cellulite on my legs.

For the record, the photos were not retouched. When Judith told me her friends didn't believe my legs were really that smooth, I'd never been more flattered in my life. As I've mentioned, my hindquarters are decent, thanks to genes and twenty years of on-again off-again running. My squishy stomach, obscured in the published portfolio, had dimples enough for both legs, plus a pair of arms. If the women of the Well got a glimpse of some of the deflated tire shots, they wouldn't doubt their veracity.

Would I trade my smooth thighs for a tiny waist? In a heartbeat. I'd trade my curly hair for straight. My fair skin for olive. My big feet for petite. My mannish hands for dainty. Since that wasn't possible, as an alternative, I could accept the things I cannot change, find the courage to change the things I can, and have the wisdom to know the difference.

Body Image Anonymous. An idea whose time has come?

The most out-of-the-blue call post-ultimate-reveal was from two very nice women who organized charity events for a temple in Short Hills. I knew the temple well, an ark-shaped building less than a mile from my childhood home. I'd gone to Sunday school there, attended dozens of bar and bat mitzvahs inside those walls. The women—K. and D.—were on the hunt for a keynote speaker for a spring luncheon fund-raiser, a few months away. It was their association's biggest annual event. Hundreds of women, corporate sponsors, whole ball of kosher wax. D. said she'd been following my work in magazines for years. She'd seen the *Self* article and thought it'd be swell to have me, a native Short Hillian, come talk to the temple ladies about my efforts to overcome bad body image. Plus, they offered to pay me two thousand dollars to do it. Was I available?

First thought: I knew my bad body image would be worth something someday.

Second thought: If I do hardcore Atkins before the luncheon, then I'll . . .

Third thought: *Whoa, girl.* I'd made a vow. There would

be no dieting for specific events. No dieting on deadline. No dieting at all.

Attempting not to sound overeager, I said, "*Two thousand bucks??! Yeah, baby! That's what I'm talkin' about! I am there.*"

D. arranged for Liz, my oldest friend (we'd done summer camp, the Millburn public school system, and Condé Nast together), who still lived in Short Hills and was a temple member, to introduce me at the lunch. Five minutes after D. and I hung up, Liz called, and we laughed at the heresy of me, a flamingly secular Jew, speaking to the temple women about the self-perpetuating failure of dieting, while we all picked at salads, dressing on the side.

"This is a fancy lunch," said Liz. "Most of the spring selections at Neiman Marcus will be on display."

"So jeans and a T-shirt would be considered dressing down?" I asked, instantly feeling the usual anxiety about having to go shopping, try on clothes, look in a three-way mirror.

"For two thousand dollars, you can buy a new dress," she said.

12

OUR WARDROBES, OURSELVES

You might've heard the axiom: Women wear 10 percent of their wardrobe 90 percent of the time. It was certainly true for me—because I could fit into only 10 percent of mine. My closet didn't contain just fat clothes and skinny clothes. I had the fat-fat selection, the medium-fat, the bordering on average, average, slightly below average, and the skinny items I hadn't worn for over a decade. These pieces had become "goal" clothes. Instead of inspiring me, however, they became wrinkled reminders of my failure.

Most women, at a tender age, learn from their mothers about the joy of shopping and the special satisfaction of finding the perfect outfit. My initiation into the ritual was a nightmare. I still get the shakes, remembering Mom, Alison, and me in the communal dressing room at Bloomingdale's, circa 1975. Alison slipped into pleated wool skirts, ivory silk blouses, and bell-bottoms effortlessly, looking scrawny and stylish. She smiled and twirled, falling in love with shopping, an enduring love for her. While she posed in the mirror, I was over there in the corner, trying to wedge myself into gauchos and lumpy cowl-neck sweaters. Nothing fit right or looked halfway decent. The saleslady sighed heavily and said, "I'll get that in a larger size." Mom frowned disapprovingly. "It's the largest size in juniors," she complained. "We'll have to go to misses." I had to wait for another armful of things that wouldn't fit, quivering kid flesh in white panties in front of the orgy of mirrors.

Alison walked out of that chamber of horrors with a new fall wardrobe, twelve pieces, cute as hell. Me? I got a poncho. And a pair of Mary Janes.

To this day, the words "gaucho," "poncho," and "culottes" make me shudder.

Mom wised up, and left me behind when she and Alison went to Bloomingdale's. Her shopping expeditions with me began and ended at Bill's Army and Navy store for Wrangler jeans, gray or navy hoodies, and crewneck pack-of-three T-shirts in a variety of colors. If I needed a skirt or blouse for an occasion, Mom would shop without me. She'd go to a department store, come home with a few boxes, and pull the items over my head or tug them over my rump. If the pieces fit, we'd keep them. I'd put on the dress as directed, go to the party, wedding, bar mitzvah, Broadway show, or ballet. Fit was all that mattered. Style, cut, and color were not taken into account. Clothes were functional. They covered my nakedness and protected me from the cold. I was relieved not to have to go shopping. Trying on clothes made me feel fat, jealous of Alison, and embarrassed by the saleswomen. It made me feel like a disappointment to Mom.

When I got older, shopping became a leisure sport among my friends in junior high. At first, I'd beg off trips to Lord & Taylor. Later, I took an outright antifashion political stance that reeked of adolescent defiance. "Clothes are superficial. The fashion industry contributes to our consumerist society," I said. I had to eat my words (tasty!) when I went whole hog for the preppy trend. A few years later, like shedding an old skin for a new one, I traded preppy for punk. Then punk yielded to hippie chic in college. I wore the appropriate rock-and-roll uniforms and copied my friends.

When I went to work in magazines and had to dress like a professional, I was at a loss. My stylish friend Tomas took me to CP Shades to buy a few outfits. He did his best, but shapeless cotton-knit duds were not in the same universe as the finer fabrics worn by the editors of the magazine publishing world.

Again, my snotty "clothes are for silly twits" attitude kicked in. I didn't even pretend to follow fashion. I was miles behind my colleagues in my sartorial education; I could never hope to catch up. When we got wind of a designer's top-secret sample sale, all work would stop as the editors raced maniacally to get there. I'd go along to see what the fuss was about. We'd enter a warehouse or a showroom and find racks and racks of skirts, dresses, trousers, and blouses hanging riotously, strewn across the floor, piled in disarray on tables. While the editors picked through the fabric mountains, hunting for gems like miners on crack, I'd stand against the wall and stare in disbelief. A bargain made otherwise rational, intelligent women go bonkers. I simply did not get it. If clothes fit, were black, and were climate appropriate, they were okay by me.

Even clothes that should have had held sentimental value for me didn't. I hadn't personally selected them. The backless dress I wore the night I met Glenn had been picked out for me by an editor at *Mademoiselle*. The velvet dress I wore when Glenn and I got engaged was borrowed from his roommate. My two wedding dresses? The first, a hand-me-down from Alison, had had to be let out (way out) for me. I just stood there for the fittings, barely paying attention. It was white, princessy. It served its purpose.

I did choose my second wedding dress, less than two weeks before the event. Of all the items on my prewedding to-do list, I bought the dress last. If you need to ask why, you haven't been paying attention. I *hate shopping!* For moral support, I begged Steve to go to SoHo with me. He loathed shopping as much as I did and was none too happy to be dragged around the city on a sweltering August afternoon. A fashionable friend gave me a list of stores, all within a ten-block radius. We blew through one shop after another, looked around, saw nothing good, left frustrated. At a few, I tried on a dress that looked good on the hanger, hideous on me. My mood tumbled if a size twelve was tight. I eventually bought a two-hundred-dollar Nicole Miller white sheath dress. Size ten. It fit, was white, and was climate appropriate. The size and price were emotionally and financially acceptable. I exited the dressing room and showed Steve. He said, "It looks fine." I checked myself out in the mirror. The dress met my standard criteria: It didn't make me look too fat. I told the salesgirl that I'd take it. I'd only tried on the one dress.

"It's for your wedding, right?" she asked.

"Yup," I said.

"Do you want to try on a few more dresses? Just to be sure?"

I was sure enough. The frock met my needs. It was hotter than heck outside. Steve was tired. I was hungry. Buying the dress would be a huge load off my mind. Buying *any* dress would have been a relief.

I said, "This'll do, thanks."

The salesgirl said, "But for your wedding, you have to absolutely love it. It's got to be perfect."

She was just like my colleagues at *Mademoiselle*. She loved clothes. She had an emotional connection with what she put on her back, and she wouldn't be satisfied unless I did, too.

I said, "I do! I absolutely *adore* it! I *love* it! I've been searching the city for months. I'm thrilled beyond thrilled to have finally found the one perfect divine sent-from-heaven-on-the-wings-of-angels dress!"

Only then would she take my card and put the dress in a bag.

The only garments I've ever felt close to were, actually, undergarments. I've had a long love affair with underwear. It is a perplexing paradox that someone with my body image problems would be a huge fan of lingerie. Sexy panties and bras have given me what little clothingwise confidence I could claim. Lacy garments held emotional weight because they were associated with my relationships. After Glenn died, opening my underwear drawer and seeing the bras, panties, and nighties he'd loved on me hit me with a wave of grief every day. An important part of my recovery was to throw away the items that reminded me of our sex life and to stock up instead on plain panties and bras, as colorless as I felt.

When Steve and I started dating, I slowly replenished my drawer with Victoria's Secret goodies. Wearing sexy underwear again was like coming back to life. In vivid color. The rest of my wardrobe? As black as midnight.

Since the early days of J.Crew, I'd ordered most of my clothes from catalogues. Or I'd zip into a store and buy a pile of things to try on later, at home. My loathing for dressing rooms has cost me a fortune in clothes that I thought would fit and then didn't. Instead of going through the hassle of returning them, I'd shove them in my closet (more goal clothes to torment me), where they'd hang untouched for years. For my utilitarian clothing needs (i.e., all of my clothing needs), I fell into the Gap. When Old Navy stores arrived in the early 1990s, I went there instead. Same stuff, half the price. Thanks to Old Navy, the stuff I bought that didn't fit or looked bad, never to be returned or exchanged, was far less expensive. I saved hundreds!

I met Rebecca for breakfast. She hadn't seen the naked photo story yet, so I brought the magazine to show her. "Well, you've proven to the world that you can get undressed," she said. "Now you should learn how to get dressed."

I said, "You don't like what I'm wearing?"

"Jeans and a hoodie?"

"My trademark ensemble."

"That's not an ensemble," said Rebecca. "It's grabbing what's clean and throwing it on."

Exactly. "One of the benefits of not caring," I said. "I don't agonize about what to wear."

"You've obviously lost weight. Why not buy some clothes that fit? At least get a pair of nicer jeans. Or a cashmere hoodie with a shape to it," she said.

I cringed, knowing where this conversation was going. I'd had it before, with Rebecca and many others. The "pride in your appearance" conversation. The "dress like an adult" chat. I changed the subject. For once, Rebecca didn't force the issue.

But her point stuck in my head for many meals to come. I'd spent the last seven months purging my figurative closet of emotional skeletons, throwing out the mental clutter, clearing space for a new, healthy way of thinking. What of my actual closet?

I walked into it (yes, my closet is a walk-in, which many people have said was wasted on me) and turned on the light. I flipped through the hangers, examined the shelves and drawers. Ninety percent of the contents were black. That same percentage didn't fit. Black clothes were in sync with the black-and-white dieting existence, but I'd given that up months ago. My wardrobe was lagging behind. To take a further step away from that way of life, I needed to shop and dress more colorfully, too. To truly change the way I thought about my body, I would have to make alterations to its material covering as well.

Clueless how to begin, I needed help from an expert.

I first met Stacy London at *Mademoiselle*. She joined the staff as a stylist during the halcyon Elizabeth Crow years. Before Stacy's arrival, I hadn't befriended anyone in the fashion department, but she and I became instant pals. Her frank sense of humor was irresistible, and she made me howl with laughter in meetings. Since then, Stacy has gone on to well-deserved fame and fortune as the host of the hit TV show *What Not to Wear.* The show's premise is simple: Stacy and Clinton Kelly, her cohost, descend upon an unsuspecting style-challenged target, throw out all her old clothes, take her shopping for new stuff, and, in the process, transform her entire life.

If I were going to accept fashion makeover advice from *anyone,* it'd be Stacy. So I called her up and asked if she'd be willing to take a peek in my closet. "I would *love* to," she said. "It would be my absolute *pleasure.*" I could practically hear her salivating over the phone, all too eager to rip apart my lame wardrobe.

That was when I got a little nervous.

A couple of weeks later—during which time I wore the same four outfits on steady rotation, most of it gym clothes, grubby T-shirts, and jeans—Stacy arrived at my place looking smashing in a black V-neck dress, metallic thong sandals, sparkling jewelry, and a jean jacket that fit her perfectly. After giving her a tour of the rest of my apartment, I drew a deep breath and brought her to my bedroom.

But I didn't let her look in my closet—yet. I needed a little foreplay before the plunder began.

"Why should I care about fashion?" I asked.

"I hear the defiance in your voice," said Stacy, sitting on the edge of my bed. "And I agree with it. Fashion *is* superficial. Following fashion does make you materialistic. The fashion industry definitely takes advantage of the attitude that if you don't get this bag or dress or shoe, you're socially unacceptable."

"Uh, aren't you part of the fashion industry?" I asked.

"Not anymore," she said. "What I've learned on five years of *What Not to Wear* is that fashion has nothing to do with personal style. Fashion makes women feel insecure. Personal style gives women power. Personal style is derived from you, not from a magazine or a designer. When you dress according to your personal style—which we're going to sort out for you today—you will respect yourself like you can't even begin to imagine."

"You, meaning women in general?" I said.

"You, meaning *you,* Val Frankel," she said. "I've known you for over ten years, and you've never even tried to dress in a way that reflects who you are."

"I am who I am, regardless of what I wear," I said, sounding like that defensive adolescent I used to be.

Stacy nodded knowingly. She'd come up against the style-reluctant before. "Why should your daughters do well in school?" she asked. "Because it determines where they go to college and what kind of job they'll get. It keeps their options open. Creating a personal style is exactly the same thing. Your look is visual currency. If you want to look like a slacker in flip-flops"—she pointed at my Old Navy rubber thongs—"that's what the world will assume you are. People make snap judgments. They make subconscious judgments. If you have only one chance to telegraph a message via the way you dress, why not make it a good impression?"

I trotted out an old argument. "The only thing a highly styled person telegraphs is that she cares about clothes more than important things."

"You have a beautiful apartment, Val," said Stacy, suddenly off topic. "Where did you get that desk?"

She was referring to my George Nelson art deco desk that I found after years of searching antique stores on Atlantic Avenue in Brooklyn. I told her the story of my joy upon finding it. Stacy asked, "And these rugs. Where'd you get them?"

My Persian rugs were purchased at a warehouse sale at ABC Carpet. I waited months and months for the prices to come down to an acceptable range. I must have looked at three hundred rugs before I chose the beautiful wool and silk magic carpets that cover my bedroom floor. I listened to myself wax rhapsodical about my home decor for a spell, and then I said, "You're trying to trick me, aren't you?"

Stacy laughed. "You obviously care about your surroundings. The first thing you did when I got here was to give me the tour. You take pride and joy in the first impression your home design says about you. Yet you don't care about the impression *you* make?"

"Got it."

"Wouldn't it be fabulous to impress people without having to say something smart or write a single word?" she asked.

It would indeed. "Yes."

"I've done two hundred shows," she said. "I've worked with men, women, and kids of every body type. I've *been* every body type! From being so small I had to shop in the children's section to wearing a size eighteen, and every size in between. I'm guessing you think you can't use the power of personal style because of your body size. Body size has nothing to do with it. *Size doesn't matter.* You can look and feel great at any size. You don't have to spend oodles of money. Style has no price points. Grace, personality, and intelligence are the things you love about yourself on the inside—and you can love them about yourself on the outside, too."

I liked what she was saying, in theory, but I still couldn't get over what I'd always thought, that clothes were insignificant. Furniture, on the other hand, was permanent, big, with intrinsic value that could be passed from one generation to the next. Furniture was art.

"You love objects," she said. "Your sparkly kitchen counter. Your acrylic toilet seats. You've found a way to create joy in the everyday. You can look at your red walls and feel good. You can also look at yourself in a flattering red dress and feel good. You styled your home for joy. And you're going to start styling yourself for joy, too. Look, I'm not delusional. Obviously, a great shirt isn't going to end the war. It won't cure disease or stop global warming. But, in general, fashion can make an impact. I talk about style as visual currency. Visual currency is nonverbal communication. When a woman walks out in the morning with confidence—she loves her heels, her dress, she thinks she looks great—her day will be better. She'll be nicer to the people she interacts with. They'll have a better day. And so on, and so on. You're creating joy and spreading it around. Is that insignificant?"

Obviously not. Spreading joy is my usual aim anyway. I write comedy, after all, and strive to make my family and friends happy.

"It has to start with how you feel about yourself," said Stacy. "You've had a lifetime of looking in the mirror and asking, 'Do I look fat in this?' Go out and buy clothes that make you *feel* great. I can teach you techniques for dressing your frame—not Giselle's frame—and finding things that are slimming, that highlight what you like, that camouflage what you don't. But only you know what makes you *feel* great. Mainly, it's about allowing yourself to feel and be beautiful in a way that celebrates your entire person. I can definitely think of a few things that are less superficial than that. People spend thousands of dollars and hours in therapy, but there's a lot to be said for putting on a pretty dress."

My inner feminist reflexes kicked in. I had to question this line of thought. As women, weren't we too complicated to let the simplicity of looking pretty nourish our souls?

A Vassar philosophy major, Stacy had obviously done a lot of thinking about all this. "Women our age are fighting a tougher battle than our mothers and grandmothers," she said. "They fought to be seen by men as more than decorative sexual objects, for the right not to be judged on their looks alone. Our generation is supposed to be CEOs, mothers, wives, expert lovers, have perfect bodies, run marathons, make a million dollars, be gourmet chefs, swing a golf club, never eat, never get tired. Men of any generation have never been asked to do what feminism asks of us. We are multitaskers, but we're not superhuman. The standard for what is expected of us, and what we expect of ourselves, is too high. We're supposed to be all things to all people—and we wonder why we're unhappy. You, Val, have fifteen pounds of guilt and shame for not being who you think you're supposed to be. Those fifteen pounds are an anvil around your neck. You wake up in the morning and feel the heaviness before you get out of bed. It affects your day and your life. I've been there, as you know. What I'm telling you is that personal style, dressing well and caring about your clothes, is one simple way to make you feel better, to lighten the load. Why shouldn't you take advantage? Given how hard life can be, why not do the easy part?"

Hard to argue with that. But enough talking. The time had come to take every scrap of clothing out of my closet and pile it on the bed.

Almost immediately, Stacy recognized one of my big problems. "I can't tell you how many closets I've decimated that were full of cheap crap that people bought without trying on," she said. She saw the telltale tags on a skirt and threw it on the floor. "Trash pile," she said.

She held up an ankle-length linen skirt I'd never worn. I said, "That was a hand-me-down from a friend."

She checked the tag. "It's a size four."

I shrugged.

She balled up the skirt and said, "This is never going to fit you. Why is it here? It reminds you of what you think is a personal failure. It's emotional baggage." Onto the trash pile. "And what's this?"

"A skirt I got at Daffy's," I said.

"It's a size fourteen," she said. "Why have you kept it? To remind yourself of having once been that big? So you'll see it and get that ick feeling? Another reminder of your perceived failure. It's bigger than the size four, but it might as well be the same skirt." It went flying into the trash.

A dress, black. I said, "I bought it for a job interview."

"Never buy something new right before a special occasion,"

she said. "You'll wear it once and never again. Say you need a summer dress for a wedding. You go out the day before and assume you'll find the perfect thing. But you won't, and you have to settle. Take the time to make a list of basics—a job interview suit, a summer dress, a winter coat—and spend an hour a week shopping. You might find a suit at the store where you expected to find the dress. If you have a list and work to acquire what you need, you won't wind up making a snap decision on a mistake. And this dress is a mistake."

"Hey, I like that dress!" I protested. It was ten years old. And I'd only worn it, maybe, twice.

"Val, it's too short!"

"I'm accentuating the positive," I said, patting my thigh.

"Okay, it's a good instinct to emphasize and de-emphasize. You still have to see the whole picture. What you tend to do, Val, is wear tiny miniskirts and big boxy oversized sweaters that make you look like a tomato on a pair of toothpicks."

That made me laugh. She was absolutely right. "Instead," said Stacy, throwing the dress on the floor, "you can even out the top and bottom halves with a longer hemline and fitted tops."

My sweater collection: "Needs to be on antidepressants. Black, black, pilly black, faded black." Fling, fling, fling, flung. "You go for saggy weaves because you think it hides your boobs, but knits are heavy and clingy and make your boobs look even bigger. They're all oversized, which adds bulk and clings at the same time."

A black cashmere turtleneck: "This would look better on Peyton Manning."

A wool crewneck: "This gives brown a bad name."

A sand-colored cable knit. I said, "Hey, my mother bought that for me."

"Your mother hasn't done you any fashion favors," she said. "Keep her out of the shopping equation."

Good point. My mom was hardly style-savvy. We teased her for wearing the same Ferragamo boots for forty years. Both my parents spend hardly any money on clothes, diverting the cash to bigger purchases like houses, cars, antiques, travel. I'd picked up my spending style from them, as well as all my mom's faulty instincts about fashion. Her own wardrobe of low-rent bland neutrals seemed designed to conceal and hide—not trouble areas, but herself, from the world.

One article after another was thrown on the discard pile. Stacy said, "Man, you sure do like Old Navy. This shirt even says 'Old Navy' on the front. Talk about not being invested in your clothes. All this is crap! It has no intrinsic or emotional value. No wonder you don't take care of it. By the way, you need a lint brush. There's no reason things hanging should be covered in cat hair."

Old Navy: No longer the official sponsor of this book.

"You have to invest in your clothes," she added. "Increase the intrinsic value to increase the emotional value. Instead of five shirts from Old Navy, get two from Anthropologie. They'd last longer, look better. Think of it this way: You don't buy stocks because they're cheap. You buy stocks because of their potential increase in value. Do the same with clothes."

A gray short-sleeved knit sweater that I'd worn to Glenn's funeral: "Talk about emotional baggage," she said. "Do you even like it?" Not really. Fling.

A shirt with a high neckline: "Wrong."

A linen striped shirt: "Tugs across the chest, and the stripes make your tits look enormous."

A black print sundress that I wore during both my pregnancies: "You're not pregnant now, are you? Stop wearing maternity clothes. Better than the dress, you have the kids. And the kids are more flattering."

A pair of plaid kilts: "Oh, Gawd! I remember these from *Mademoiselle*. They're way too short! A sixteen-year-old can't wear skirts this mini."

"You remember what I wore *twelve years ago?*"

"I have a photographic fashion memory," said Stacy. "I also had a special fascination with your clothes. You were a high-profile person at the magazine, way up on the masthead, and yet you dressed like an intern."

Ouch.

In an hour of trashing, Stacy threw out everything she'd picked up. Nothing, as she said, had any connection to who I was. I asked, "How do I rate, in terms of being emotionally disconnected to my clothes?"

"Off the charts," she said. "What I see here is someone who has never had a sense of self in how she dresses. It's all beyond utilitarian, lifeless, and it says nothing about you. It's upsetting, really. Not so much that your clothes don't fit and aren't flattering, but they're devoid of any sense of you. Your passion and humor and intelligence. There is no link between who you are and how you dress. I'm guessing the disconnect started a long time ago, when you looked in the mirror and felt unhappy."

Hello, Bloomingdale's communal dressing room. "My hatred of shopping was formed early on."

"That is so sad. You've missed a lot," said Stacy. No ironic tone there. She felt sorry for me. I was starting to feel sad for myself. I *had* missed out on a lot—female bonding over shoes, relating to shopping scenes in books and movies, creating an outer image to match my inner.

The pillage continued. Item after item was deemed off size, a bad color, an unflattering cut, stained, ripped, cheap. She asked, "When you walk into your closet, what do you feel?"

I felt . . . happy?

"You feel like it's a torture chamber of bad memories, personal failings, and sad, ugly options," said Stacy. "Nothing here adds joy to your life. Your closet should make you feel giddy, like you're surrounded by beauty. It should be your happy place, giving you a sense of safety and competence. The same way you feel about your apartment. You can do this, Val. You designed your house as a haven and shelter. Your closet can be a sanctuary, too."

The size ten black leather jeans. I said, "Hold on. I want to keep those. I used them as a weight benchmark."

She mulled it over. "I have a pair of leather jeans, too. By the time they come back into fashion, we'll be too old to wear them. Try them on for me." I did. They fit comfortably. Not tight, but not loose either. I hadn't weighed myself since I'd been not-dieting. Nor had I tried on the leather jeans. Going by fit, I'd lost around ten pounds.

Stacy must've noticed that I suddenly looked pleased when I put them on. "Okay, you can keep them," she said. "But here's how to handle it. You make a choice to hold on to only one thing to use as a benchmark. They're not goal pants. Or a symbol of failure. They're a gauge. These jeans can be the way to track your size, to keep you honest, so you can't lie to yourself. But they can't be used for psychological torture. Let's say you can try them on once every three months."

When the pillaging ended, the trash pile on the carpet was higher than the bed. Only two neatly folded (by Stacy) stacks remained: my jeans and my gym clothes. I had a few tanks left ("for layering"), a couple of dresses ("get them re-hemmed"), and my pj's. We didn't have time to go through coats or shoes, but suffice it to say, I needed to restock the larder in both of those categories as well. A final comment, regarding footwear: "You have six pairs of rubber flip-flops," she said. "Buy some real sandals."

We stuffed the discarded items into large green garbage bags while Stacy rattled off my Basics Shopping List of items and stores.

- Two pairs of dark-wash jeans. Straight leg or slight flare. Lucky Brand, Red Engine.
- Three short blazers. Hip length, short lapel, three buttons to de-emphasize the chest and tummy. Banana Republic.
- New sweaters. Light- or medium-weight wools, preferably cashmere, for layering with tanks and shirts, in saturated jewel tones and soft neutrals like navy, brown, and gray. V-necks. Three-quarter or full-length sleeve. J.Crew.
- Two suits. One skirt, one pant. Brown pinstripe or navy glen plaid. Three-season tropical-weight

wool. Pencil skirt or A-line, to top of knee. Banana Republic, DKNY, Theory.
- Blouses. Cotton broadcloth and silk, yes; knit cotton, no. Empire waist or tunics with V-neck. Side zippers, yes; buttons across the boobs, no. Big, bold patterns, jewel tones, and soft neutrals, yes; tiny prints, no. Anthropologie, Zara.
- T-shirts. Fitted for layering with sweaters and jackets. Bright colors, V-neck, size medium. *Not large.* J.Crew, Banana Republic, Only Hearts.
- Three summer dresses. Wrap dresses, fitted sheaths with V-necks. To knee or just below knee. Soft neutrals or bold, bright prints. Embellishments: beading and embroidery. Ella Moss, Searle, Diane von Furstenberg.
- Three pairs of trousers. Straight leg or slight flare; low or at waist. DKNY, Banana Republic.

Stacy's price points were midrange. I decided to spend two thousand dollars on a new wardrobe, the same amount that had dropped into my lap from the temple ladies (easy come, easy go). I decided to forget about suits and trousers until the fall and get dresses, skirts, and blouses for spring. Along with my shopping list (which didn't include shoes and accessories: "Let's start with remedial stuff before moving to the advanced class," she said), Stacy had some rules of thumb for shopping.

1. **Forget size.** "Focusing on size is psychological torture," said Stacy. "The important thing isn't the number. It's

whether the cut is flattering on your body. Also, there is no consistency with sizes from designer to designer and store to store. A six at one place might be a twelve at another. You haven't gained an ounce, but by walking next door, you've gone up—or down—three sizes. If the six looks great, buy it. If the twelve looks great, buy it. No one can see the number but you. And if it bugs you, cut it out."

2. **Try on everything**. "Even if you get two of the same shorts in different colors, try on *both* pairs. Do not buy anything until you're sure it fits."

3. **Make friends with a tailor**. "Manufacturers produce thousands and thousands of the same item in a factory. It will never fit every single person exactly right. No two human bodies are identical. There is no perfect size eight or ten or twelve. If you spend thirty-five dollars on a shirt and add ten dollars for a tailor, the shirt will look like a hundred bucks. Men always have their suits tailored. Why should women settle for less?"

4. **Trust salespeople**. "You, Val, are in a style rut. More like a ditch, but whatever. You need to break out of it. Ask a salesperson or personal shopper at Saks or Neiman Marcus to steer you in new directions and help you find clothes that are flattering for you. I know you have bad childhood memories about salespeople, but you're all grown up now. Get over it."

We returned the tiny piles of clothes to my closet. I'd have to walk my kids to school naked tomorrow, since I had nothing to wear—literally. We hauled the Hefty bags down the stairs of my building and out to my car. We loaded them into the trunk. Next stop, Salvation Army.

"You better not sneak out any of those sweaters," she said.

I laughed (since I'd been thinking of doing just that). "I have to let it all go. And when I say 'all,' I don't mean just the clothes."

"I promise you, Val, if you can find even one article of clothing that makes you *feel* great, you'll discover a dimension of joy you didn't think possible. I'm not sure you're ready for the depth of emotion. It's big."

"I know you're right," I said. "And I'm so grateful you came over today. Obviously, I needed to do this."

"My pleasure, I mean it," she said. "There are so many people in the world who don't recognize how beautiful they are until someone shows them."

That did it. I cried. Couldn't help it. It'd been building. Thinking about the decades of disconnect, or neglect, realizing how little respect I'd shown myself and the world through my clothes. I suddenly understood why people bawled on *What Not to Wear* every week. Stacy cried, too. We cried together, on the street, by my car with the two huge garbage bags in the trunk.

We composed ourselves, laughing and saying good-bye. Stacy told me to call her with questions. "Remember," she said. "Forget about looking thin. It's not how you look, but how you feel."

The next day, I planned on going to Banana Republic to begin my new shopping life. Maggie insisted on going with me, "to make sure you follow Stacy's rules." When Lucy heard that, she said she wanted to come, too. It'd be a mother and her two daughters in the dressing room all over again, minus the clucking, loaded sighs, and disapproving looks.

By all indications, my bad shopping habits hadn't rubbed off on my girls. They were fashion junkies, almost from birth. When they tried on clothes in dressing rooms, I told them they looked adorable in everything. They did! They're both beautiful, as I remind them all the time. Conventional wisdom dictates that parents shouldn't do that, but I knew there were worse things a mother could say to her daughters in dressing rooms.

As we walked to BaRe after school, I thought, "Here we are. Going shopping. Just like normal people."

We entered the store, and I had to forcibly steer myself away from the sale rack. I was not going to automatically buy the cheapest, blackest, biggest whatever. I was going to browse. We started pulling things off the racks. Twenty items, in Stacy-approved colors and cuts. Then we hauled the lot to a sizable dressing room. Maggie and Lucy sat on the floor as I tried on each piece. If something didn't fit, it was a no, obviously. If Maggie or Lucy was iffy, it was a no. If I was iffy, hell no. If a shirt fit and we all liked it, then I had to decide whether wearing it evoked emotion in my heart. Did it make me feel joy?

This was the tricky part. For the first few tentative yeses, I wasn't sure what I felt, except a smug satisfaction that I was fitting into a lot of size eights (on the bottom), which was a nice surprise.

When I tried on a pair of gray linen shorts, a white tank,

and a cranberry summerweight sweater with a deep V-neck, Maggie said, "Love."

Lucy said, "Totally."

I appraised the outfit. I smiled, liked it. Especially the bright sweater. Then a faint hum rose in my ears. It got louder as I turned for the side view. I said, "Do you hear that?"

"What?" the girls asked.

"Forget it."

I tried on a brown empire-waist dress with embroidery at the hem and a V-neck.

Maggie said, "It's too baggy. What size is it?"

"Large," I said.

"You're not supposed to wear large," recited Maggie. "Stacy *said* medium." I got the feeling I was in for a lot of "Stacy *said*" from now on.

"But the boobs," I said, turning to the sides. Mediums on the bottom were fine, but I needed more room on top.

Maggie stood up and said, "I'm getting a medium."

She left the dressing room and came back with a smaller size. I tried it on. The medium did fit better, even across the chest. I surveyed the image in the mirror, liking what I saw. Loving what I saw. The hum started again in my head. Not as faint.

Lucy said, "Do a twirl."

I twirled. It really did look great. Flattering empire waist, hemline right at the knee. Wide shoulder straps and a bronzy brown that set off my hair and eyes. Okay, the hum was loud in my head now. I would have to recognize it for what it was: an auditory manifestation of emotion. Was it joy? I wasn't sure, but it got louder the longer I wore the dress.

Maggie said, "Definite yes for me."

Lucy said, "Me, too."

The dress cost nearly two hundred bucks. I'd never spent that much on a single item of clothing. I could get three dresses at Old Navy for . . .

Stacy *said* I had to go for quality. One beautiful dress that made me feel good was worth a hundred pieces of crap I'd wear once and never again.

I bought it. And the sweater, the tank, the shorts, a shirt, and a top. I spent over four hundred dollars. Maggie seemed particularly excited that I was slapping down the card. She knew that if I turned into a shopper, it'd mean more clothes for her (she turned out to be right about that). A week later, I went back to Banana Republic to return the top. After the initial enthusiasm for it, I'd changed my mind. And it cost seventy dollars! Over the years, I hadn't returned hundreds of dollars' worth at Target, Old Navy, and Daffy's. I was learning. Stacy *said* I had to think of clothes as stocks. If I bought a bad stock, I dumped it. If I thought twice about a top, I would return it.

A few days later, after dropping off the kids at school, I went into Manhattan, to Fifth Avenue in Greenwich Village, and was amazed to find three of my Stacy-approved stores right next to each other! I wondered if she'd planned that. I went from Zara to J.Crew to Anthropologie and spent five hours (!) trying on scores of blouses, T-shirts, skirts, dresses, jackets, and pants. My buy percentage was about one in four. Since I had an idea of what to look for—stylewise and emotionally—I was very selective. Even if something looked right, I wouldn't buy it unless I heard the hum, felt the love. I didn't get hung up on sizes.

This will seem like stating the obvious to most: Shopping was *fun*! I shopped 'til I dropped. My bags were heavy on my arms. And the salespeople were so nice! At J.Crew, they gave me bottles of water and hung my selections in a reserved dressing room. While I waited in there, they brought me different colors and sizes of dresses and skirts. It was a pleasure, and I found myself feeling pampered, respected, and itching to spend, spend, spend. I knew the girls worked on commission and were paying special attention to me because I had a mad-shopper look in the eye. I didn't care! I dropped over a thousand dollars that day.

I got home and arranged my new purchases in my closet. I modeled all of it for Steve, who said the same exact thing about each one: "Great!" (He really couldn't care less about clothes.) I modeled for the girls later, Maggie gasped when I put on one outfit from J.Crew, a navy flowy skirt and a white tank. She hugged me and said, "Mom, you look so cute!"

That was joy, right there. Not because I looked cute, but because I'd made my daughter proud of me. I'd become more of who she'd like me to be, and who she'd like to be. Why shouldn't role modeling include clothes modeling? And looking cute?

I proceeded to look smokin' cute the whole next day in that outfit. I strutted around Brooklyn Heights like I owned it. At a Montague Street boutique, I bought myself a pair of high-heeled sandals. And a purse to match the shoes. And a pair of earrings. I was in free-spending mode and knew I'd have to stop soon.

Until then, I'd drown in the joy. And once I reached my two-thousand-dollar limit (any minute now), I'd still have all the clothes! Stacy had been right. Two weeks after her visit, I understood what she'd been trying to tell me. Shopping wasn't a values dilemma. By dressing better, I was making a better impression—on strangers, acquaintances, the kids. Mainly, on myself.

I can think of a lot of things less valuable than that.

13

SAVE THE DATE

When Steve and I first started planning our wedding, people asked why I was bothering with the formality when we could just be together without involving the government. A couple of reasons: For one thing, I already knew that marriage was a comfortable, secure, convenient domestic arrangement. Also, the kids wanted us to be legally bound.

So we got married. A year later, Maggie announced that she didn't like the sound of "stepfather." She wanted a "father-father." The girls and I talked about Glenn every day. There were photos of him all over our apartment. We visited Glenn's grave, went to his parents in Florida every year, and saw his brother's family regularly. Maggie knew she had a dead father-father. But she wanted one here on earth as well.

I'd heard stories about people in our circumstances pursuing adoption. As legal procedures go, it wouldn't be too awful. The more we talked about it, the more it made sense. As my husband only, Steve had no legal rights to the kids. He couldn't give approval for an emergency medical procedure if I were unavailable. If I died while the girls were minors, he'd have no claim to them. There could be agonizing complications about inheritance, where they'd live, who would raise them.

My parents and sister applauded the adoption idea, for these reasons and to further solidify us as a family. I brought it up to Glenn's parents when they came to New York for a visit. The conversation went smoother than I thought it would. The idea made them sad, understandably, but they were happy for me to have found a man I trusted enough to adopt the girls.

It'd been two years since that uncomfortable talk, and yet we'd taken no steps toward making it legal. Nothing had happened. Steve hadn't brought it up since the initial flurry of conversation about it. Neither had Maggie, who, in the intervening years, had moved on to middle school with other things (clothes, gossip, the Sims) on her mind. But I still thought about the adoption often—every time I filled out a camp form or parental authorization for a class trip. Even though Steve had been raising the kids for years, he wasn't legally authorized to sign a permission slip.

I had a referral for a lawyer. The info was on a stickie on my desktop. Had been for years. It'd be easy to pick up the phone, set the wheels in motion. It had to be done. And yet, I didn't do it.

What was keeping me from making the call? The girls had thrived under our joint care. Steve was an amazing dad. He was far more involved in the girls' day-to-day lives than any other father I knew. His evening rehearsal and perfor-mance schedules made it possible for Steve to schlep the girls to karate and piano lessons—and he was glad to do it.

A bachelor until he was fifty, Steve had assumed he would

never have children. Now that he was up to his ears in Bagel
Bites, sleepover parties, juice pouches, Nickelodeon, and
math homework, he appreciated the hectic joy of living with
kids more than the average dad. More than the average
mom. The girls adored him. Lucy, who was almost two years
old when Glenn died, had considered Steve her father for
years already. Maggie and Steve bonded over music. For the
last two seasons, Maggie had sung in the chorus of Steve's
opera company. They gossiped about the other singers and
talked in the language of music to each other, which made
my tone-deaf heart sing. Steve attended every recital, game,
and play. When the second graders recited "The Midnight
Ride of Paul Revere," I watched the other dads in suits
checking their watches, tolerating the demand on their time,
wondering when they could slip away. And there was Steve,
in the front row, grinning, hanging on every word, giving
Lucy the thumbs-up, applauding the loudest when it was
over. He won the gold star for showing up, being there, not
losing his patience (as I often did), not yelling (as I did), and
enjoying (almost) every minute of the unexpected parental
turn his life had taken. He deserved to be their legal father, as
much as the girls deserved to be his legal daughters.

Perhaps I'd avoided calling a lawyer due to logistics. The
adoption would cost several grand. The paperwork would be
abundant. I'd have to go to notaries, find documents, have
things sealed and signed, get statements, schedule appointments with court counselors and judges. Then again, I'd
faced legal paperwork before, when Glenn died, and when
Steve and I got a prenup. I'd made the time and put up the
money then. Surely the adoption—a happy reason to bring

lawyers into your life—would mitigate the annoyance of paperwork, and the time and money spent.

All marital problems, deconstructed, are about trust. If my hesitation about adoption wasn't about the kids or the hassle, then it had to be about trust.

Steve had had his own trust issues, early on. He refused to sublet his Manhattan apartment, even after we got married. He said he needed a place for all his stuff. We both knew that apartment was a safety net, an escape option for him. For me, it was an affront, an insult, a one-bedroom-sized hole in his commitment to our marriage. And then there was the money suck. He spent thousands a month on his bachelor pad, despite the fact that he was never there. I argued that money would be better spent on the Brooklyn mortgage, on groceries, on *anything*.

Initially, I accepted his decision and found ways to rationalize it as a good thing. Before long, though, his keeping the apartment became a problem. We fought about it. A lot. He had a dry spell professionally and needed a loan to pay his rent. I wouldn't give it to him. He considered my refusal hostile and mean-spirited. I said I couldn't in good conscience flush hard-earned money down the toilet. We reached a stalemate. Our fights drove us into therapy. We auditioned two marriage counselors. As soon as Steve and I explained the root of our problem—that bloody apartment—both of them turned to him and asked, "Why do you think you can't let it go?" We ended up picking a therapist who looked and sounded eerily like Steve's mother. She set him straight. After three sessions, Steve found a subletter, and the apartment conflict was gone.

When he realized how much of an albatross that place—and what it represented—had been, Steve was glad to have been pushed into giving it up. Correspondingly, at the start of our second year of marriage, we had a second honeymoon period. He'd conquered his doubt. But, as my hesitation about the adoption demonstrated, I hadn't dealt with mine. In an ideal world, each spouse would face his or her issues before they said, "I do." Steve and I were both a bit more plodding. I had yet to ease the persistent doubt in my mind about his "lose the belly" comment from years before. Even worse, I'd kept my anxiety a secret.

It bears mentioning that Steve never repeated the criticism, although I certainly invited him to. ("How do I look in these pants?" "Don't you think my stomach looks better?" "My crunches are really paying off, don't you think?") Any sane woman would have forgiven and forgotten. If we went to therapy again over this, the shrinks would surely turn to me and say, "Why do you think you can't let it go?" We'd need more than three sessions to address that.

In the beginning of our relationship, I'd loved reinventing myself. I could portray myself as someone who'd never been harassed about my weight, who was carefree and confident about my body. But that game of pretend was impossible to perpetuate. The streaks of distrust about his attraction ran through my mind like marbling through steak. I couldn't seal our family's future legally via adoption (a vastly bigger commitment than marriage) unless we cleared up this last hanging doubt. Steve would have to get a crash course in my body image history, and he'd have to understand why that comment he made years ago rattled me to the core.

I did not look forward to having this conversation. Since there was no good time to reveal your insecurities to the man you loved, I chose a quiet, peaceful moment. Steve was lying on the bed, resting between homework hour and dinner. I sat at my computer, playing Snood.

"Steve, you asleep?" I asked.

"Not quite," he said, eyes closed.

I loved watching him in this half-conscious state. When he was relaxed, he had the skin of a thirty-year-old. His lips pursed slightly, and I smiled at the sight. Steve was a damned handsome guy, and watching him at ease was one among many small pleasures I took in his presence.

"So listen," I said. "Remember the night we decided to get married?"

He said, "Sort of."

"You were just back from a tour," I said. "We hadn't seen each other in a few weeks. We made mad, passionate love for hours and hours. And then we decided to stay together forever."

He nodded, "It was a midwestern tour."

"Do you remember that you asked me to lose the stomach bulge?" I asked.

"Vaguely," he said.

"You did," I said.

"Okay."

"Well, I didn't like that," I said. "It hurt my feelings."

"Sorry," he said, turning from his back onto his side.

"Don't you feel bad that you hurt my feelings?" I asked.

He groaned and opened his eyes. "We are talking about a conversation from five and a half years ago?"

"It's still relevant."

He sat up, rearranging himself with his back to the head-board and his legs bent at the knee. He said, "I'm sorry your feelings were hurt, but they shouldn't have been. As I recall, I said it nicely enough."

So he did remember. "It's not nice to say 'lose the belly,' no matter how you couch it," I said. "Just mentioning it pushed my personal panic button. It unleashed a lifetime of bad feelings about my weight. My mother used to criticize my belly, too."

"You can't possibly be comparing me to your mother."

Indeed, Steve and Judy were polar personality opposites. "Not that you're like her, but that comment opened up a well of negative associations."

I brought him up to speed about Mom and junior high, college, my early magazine career. Telling him the stories was easier than I expected. He listened quietly but with both ears. Steve didn't make supportive or sympathetic noises. He just took it in.

When I finished, Steve shrugged. "I didn't know all that," he said. "I had no idea about your history. I thought you were happy about your stomach. You seemed to be, because you had it. If you didn't like it, I figured you'd have gotten rid of it."

I blinked in disbelief at his crazy talk. "So millions of people all over the world are happy about their fat because they haven't been able to lose it? Like they're not *trying*?"

"When we met," he said, "you gave me the immediate impression of self-assurance. You walked—you still do—with confidence. When you're working out a lot, you glide, actually. It's fun to watch. So I assumed you were pleased with yourself from top to bottom, or else you wouldn't be so confident."

I could understand his making that assumption. He was a linear-minded guy. A face-value Mainer. And, generally speaking, I did walk with a lively step. I was pretty confident— but only on the surface. Even a blind man could see that! "You must have noticed that I'm a compulsive dieter. That my weight has gone up and down over the years."

"What I notice is that you go through grumpy phases and happy phases," he said. "When you're losing weight, you tend to be cheerful and fun to be around."

"And when I'm gaining?"

"You're kind of nasty," he said. "Terse and humorless. Not at all like a jolly fat person." He smiled mischievously.

Asshole! "You're an asshole," I said. But I grinned, too.

"I'm happy when you're happy," he said. "Like husbands all over the world. What I don't get is why your mood seems to hang on miniscule weight losses. So many times, you announce that you lost five pounds, and I can barely tell. You always look pretty good. I don't have qualms about your belly anymore."

"You cared then, but don't now?" I asked. "Why?"

Steve paused to think. "Well," he said, "a person can get used to just about anything."

Shithead! "You are truly a bastard," I said, but we were both laughing now. "Seriously, what changed?"

"Well, your belly is better now," he observed correctly. "Much firmer. I have noticed that."

"Thank you, but flattery won't get you out of this. You're

going to have to explain yourself. Why did you say what you said that night?"

Steve sighed. "We were in the early stage of being physical. Your belly just got in the way. I was never focused on disliking it, but I thought we could get closer—in a purely physical sense—if it didn't come between us."

Hmmm. That actually made sense. When I was in a thinner phase, Steve really got into the full-body hugs, the frontal pressing and head-to-toe connection, as if we were fused into one four-legged package. A flatter stomach did make the connection closer.

"I get frustrated when I lose weight and you don't notice," I complained.

"Maine is one of the fattest states in the country," he said. "I grew up seeing some really massive people. Three-, four-hundred-pounders. I never considered your weight, even when it's up, to be that bad. There's fat, and then there's fat-fat. You're just not a fat-fat person. You get all excited losing five or ten pounds. It's not dramatic enough to register with me. You say you're down two dress sizes since last summer. I'm sorry, but you don't seem that different. I don't even know what two dress sizes means."

"So you'd notice only if I lost a hundred pounds," I said.

"I had no idea this was such a deep issue for you, with your mom and all this past stuff," he said. "I've noticed that you seem to care a lot about your losses and gains, but I never would have connected it to me, or anything I've said. I think I've been worshipful of your body, haven't I?"

I said, "Yes."

"I'm devoted to you," he said.

"I know."

"Then why have you been obsessing over some minor comment I made years ago when I was probably drunk?" he asked. "And why didn't you say something sooner?"

"I was embarrassed," I admitted.

"You should be," he said.

Being embarrassed about my weight obsession seemed like a step in the right direction.

He said, "Anything I say, take it at face value. I think you're a damned attractive person. When I make love to you, it's because I'm damned attracted to you."

"No matter what condition my belly is in?" I asked, one more time for good measure.

He groaned. "The belly is still here, and so am I."

"But firmer," I said.

"Definitely firmer," he agreed.

When Glenn and I were first married, I started having a recurring dream. Nothing too bizarre. A breakup scene. We'd be sitting at a café, and then he'd lower the boom, tell me he'd fallen out of love and he was leaving. The dream would continue with disjointed scenes from my new life as a divorcée. In bed alone, watching TV. Preparing meals by myself. Missing him and trying to rally my spirits. Being single wasn't so bad. I'd been there dozens of times, and I'd survived. I'd wake up and feel awesome relief to see Glenn in bed next to me. I'd punch him in the arm and say, "In my dream, you were mean to me." Glenn always apologized for the evildoings of my paranoid subconscious.

After he died, I had vivid dreams of Glenn being miraculously cured, or of our lives before he got sick, as if the cancer and death had been the dream. Maggie also had what we called "Glenn visit" dreams—visions of him descending from heaven to see what we were up to, or of him just walking in the door, whole and healthy, still her dad. The morning after, we were happy to have made a connection with the way things were, but sad that he was gone. I continued to have Glenn-returns dreams, long after Steve became enmeshed in our lives, but my reaction to having them changed. Would I still want Glenn to reappear, to walk in the door, miraculously cured?

Maggie asked, "Is it wrong to want to keep my life the way it is now?"

No eleven-year-old should have to straddle such a dilemma. I assured her that she could love Glenn's memory and still not wish for him to return. That if heaven did exist (and I wasn't saying it did) and Glenn was up there watching, he was glad we'd found someone else to love. I told myself the same thing. Even so, I still felt a twinge of guilt about wanting my life as it was now, with Steve.

I'd had dreams of Steve leaving me, too. They were eerily similar to the Glenn-breakup dreams. I was dumped, and then I'd flash to vignettes of my new lonely life. I'd wake up with a jolt, heart pounding. I'd stare at Steve sleeping next to me until I calmed down. He was still here. I wasn't alone again.

Looking at marital longevity from a practical standpoint, Steve would probably predecease me. He was eleven years older. He had a heart arrhythmia. He drank a lot of beer and never worked out (yet never gained weight, lucky bastard).

The dreams of Steve leaving didn't spring from a paranoid subconscious. They were reality-based. One husband had died on my watch. Another was likely to.

A weight obsession was a convenient distraction from bigger issues.

It was certainly easier to focus on Steve's being turned off by my stomach than to face my fear of death.

The whole point of Steve's adopting the kids was to ensure a continuation of the girls' lives here in Brooklyn in the event of my untimely death. Connecting the dots, I wondered if my legal feet-dragging was related to fear of death—not Steve's, but my own. I'd seen Glenn alive one second and dead the next. I had no idea what was in store for me or Steve. Death could happen to anyone, at any time. It would assuredly come, and it wouldn't be pretty.

That I'd wasted a single second of my time with Steve fretting about one stupid comment suddenly galled me. We had a finite number of years together. And I would be grateful for each of them. If he died first, if I died first, the living spouse had to continue, and strive for happiness for him or herself—and for *our* kids. That was the obligation of a spouse and a parent. If you couldn't meet your responsibility, you might as well be swallowed up by the earth, gone forever, never to return.

Since our talk about the belly comment, Steve started each day by wrapping me in his arms and saying, "Good morning, darling. You're not fat at all today."

When something went awry—the cat peed on Maggie's

cell phone, the kitchen fuse blew—Steve shot me a mockingly sincere look, clasped my hands tightly, and asked, "Do you think it's because of . . . *your fat*?"

When something went right—a great out-of-the-blue assignment, my lilac tree finally blooming after four years—Steve pulled me into a squeeze and asked, "How is all this happiness possible, considering . . . *you know*," and then he would glance at my midsection.

Maggie caught on to what he was doing and took to teasing me, too. It was weird at first. A sore subject for so long, it'd been co-opted by Steve and Maggie as material for improv comedy. I laughed along. The ability to laugh at yourself is a sign of higher intelligence. So, yeah, I was down with that. I teased Maggie and Steve often about their quirks (Maggie's tendency to spill whatever liquid was within reach; Steve's habit of misplacing his backpack). Why shouldn't my fat obsession be fodder for family fun? Given the choice, to cry about it or laugh, was there any doubt which was preferable? For all of us?

The mood at home palpably lifted. It made me think back to when Steve and I first connected online, crafting perfect jewels in the form of e-mails to send to each other as gifts. I summoned all my skills to sound witty, so he'd laugh and be impressed by my cleverness. In turn, I was blown away by his sense of humor. Writing those funny notes bonded us before we'd laid eyes on each other, before we finally, blissfully, laid hands on each other. Much as we loved to have sex, Steve and I loved to laugh even more. The jokes he served up after I made my big confession erased the doubt and made me fall in love with him all over again.

I realized I'd been twice blessed in marriage. First, with Glenn, an adoring husband who'd been respectful of my insecurities. Second, with Steve, my husband, my equal, who helped me overcome my insecurities by laughing about them.

Three years after we got married, six years after we sent those funny e-mails to each other, Steve and I called Barry M. Katz, Esq., to get the adoption ball rolling.

Steve asked, "Are you sure we're not rushing into this?"

"I should have done it years ago," I said, regarding the adoption, and a few other things.

14

THE PROPER WAY
TO EAT A RAT

When we last saw Sal, heroine of dozens of stories scribbled in my teenage journals, she was serving a plate of spaghetti to Z., her number-one nemesis. He waited at a beautifully set table, fork and spoon in his hands, still muddy after a triumphant soccer match. Although he was hungry enough to eat the meat of an entire elephant, he wasn't about to dive into the steaming bowl of pasta Sal had prepared. He wisely asked Y., his henchboy and Sal's number-two nemesis, to be his food taster. Worshipfully devoted to his leader, Y. obediently wound his fork around a saucy strand of spaghetti and tentatively slipped it between his thin, pale lips. He chewed, waited. Nothing happened. The food was safe.

Sal smiled as Y. and Z. greedily consumed every last string of pasta. The meal was delicious, mouthwatering. To enhance the chunky red sauce, Sal had sprinkled it liberally with parsley, oregano—and a slow-acting poison she'd concocted in her underground laboratory. When the poison finally kicked in, twenty-five years from that very moment, Y. and Z. would die instantly in a manner most grisly. Foaming at the mouth, spasmodic convulsions, eyes popping out of their sockets and rolling down the street, or the supermarket aisle, or the green of a golf course, wherever the bastards happened to be at the time. Yet again, Z. had underestimated Sal's deviousness.

The quizzical reader might wonder, why hadn't Sal used a faster-acting poison? Why delay her satisfaction by twenty-five years? Even at the impatient age of fourteen, Sal knew that revenge was a dish that people of taste preferred to eat cold.

Feeling solid after my talk with Steve, enjoying his teasing as much as I'd despised Z.'s, I felt strong and ready to take the next necessary step in my bad body image recovery.

The time had come to eat the rat.

I lost hours of sleep, fantasizing about how an encounter with Z. might go. The fantasies were similar in tone to the overwrought Sal stories from way back when. They wouldn't have been out of place in my red corduroy journal . . .

- -

Sal had had a long night. She was exhausted, but determined to see her plans through, regardless of the potentially destructive outcome. The mission was risky. But she'd been hiding in the shadows for far too long. She knew she had to face her past. Call out her dragons.

She let her head fall back on the car seat. The drive from Brooklyn to Iowa had taken its toll. She flipped down the visor to check herself in the mirror. Even after twelve hours on the road, she still looked pretty good. Fluffing her hair, Sal gave herself a pep talk.

"You can do this," she said. "Just open the car door, walk up to the house, and ring the bell."

The visor snapped back into position, Sal glanced out the car window at the house. Yellow paint peeling, shudders closed, a rusted bicycle upended on the brown lawn. It had taken her weeks of detective work to get this address. In a million years, Sal wouldn't have guessed that life had taken Z. here, to this dead-end street in a nowhere town. Her last look at him had been at high school graduation. He'd been a star that day, most likely to succeed, winning the loudest cheer from the class when the principal put the rolled-up diploma in his hand. Z. had raised his arms, cheered himself, and leapt off the low-rise stage with the grace of a gazelle.

Sal looked in her rearview mirror. Not a soul on the street. For the last five miles of her drive, she hadn't seen a single person outdoors. This was an indoors town. Doors closed, curtains drawn. Z., once a star athlete running on a green grass field, was now locked in a box. It almost made Sal feel sad. But not quite.

She took one last deep inhale, pushed open her car door, and made for the house. No bell. She knocked on the door. The contact made the door open halfway, and she could see into the house's living room. Empty pizza boxes, beer bottles, overflowing ashtrays assaulted her nostrils. She had to take a step back from the smell.

"Who's there?" barked a voice, smoke-ravaged and surly.

"Hello?" asked Sal. "I'm looking for Z. I'm an old . . . friend . . . of his from high school."

The door swung wide open, and a man appeared in the doorway. A savage stench radiated from him, and tears rose in Sal's eyes. She blinked them back and tried to breathe through her mouth.

"Z.?" she asked.

"Yeah?" he replied. Somewhere around the eyes, he looked like

his former self. Everything else had changed. The once charismatic jock with long lean legs and flowing brown hair that bounced when he ran had turned into a bald, bandy-legged troll in a soiled wife-beater T-shirt and plaid shorts belted under a rotund beer belly.

"I'm Sal, from Short Hills. We went to school together."

"Sal," he said, nodding. "Of course, I remember you. BELCH. Oops. Sorry about that."

He seemed genuinely embarrassed. Sal grimaced but asked, "May I come in?"

"Please!" he said, changing from surly to welcoming. "I can't believe this. It's so freaking weird that you're here."

Sal stepped into the house. The stink closed in. The house hadn't been aired out in months, if ever. Z. didn't seem ashamed that he lived in a hole. She said, "I should have called before I came."

"I have to get my wife," he said. "Betsy! Betsy! Get in here! You're not going to believe this."

Z. turned back to her, grinning. His two front teeth were missing. She must have reacted. He said, "Oh, yeah, my teeth. They got kicked out in a college soccer game. It was the last time I played." She detected wistfulness in his voice. But then he yelled, "Betsy! Get your fat ass down here, now."

Sal smiled nervously, looking around the room. Her eyes trailed from one stained, tattered piece of furniture to the next. Spotted gray carpet, water marks on the ceiling, dust-covered lampshades—and, on an armchair in the corner, a person. A girl. A fat girl, around thirteen or fourteen. She sat in the chair, reading a novel, in her own world, ignoring or unaware of the fact that a stranger had entered the room.

"Oh, that's just Tracy," he said. "My daughter."

He spoke without paternal pride, as if his own child were an after-

thought. Sal felt her pulse quicken. She wondered if this was what an anxiety attack felt like. If she fainted on the floor, she wondered, would she get fleas?

"What the hell do you want?" screeched a voice from deeper in the house. And then a female creature appeared in a doorway off the living room. A wild-eyed plus-size filthy blonde. The wife. Betsy. In one hand, she held a greasy turkey leg. In her other hand, she was holding a paperback book.

Z. said, "I fucking told you I knew Sal."

The wife dropped the turkey leg on the floor, where it landed with a squishy thud. She flung herself at Sal, moving across the room with the speed of a woman half her size.

"Holy shit!" squealed Betsy, staring into Sal's astonished face. "I'm your biggest fan!" Betsy held up a tattered copy of one of Sal's novels and waved it overhead.

Sal blinked in astonishment. The fans of her novels were few in number, but fierce in their loyalty. Apparently, Z.'s wife was one of them.

"Z. always told me the two of you were, like, best friends in high school," she said. "I've got all your books. You have to sign them! Come on, this way."

Betsy led Sal into the couple's squalid bedroom. Sal signed the stack of books while listening to the lady of the house explain how she'd always had her doubts that Z. and Sal had been friends, how he'd promised for years to arrange a meeting, and how shocked she was that he'd finally come through.

"He's been a pretty huge disappointment," Betsy admitted to Sal. "I mean, just look at him! He can't hold a job. We're broke. He drinks too much. He's got no friends, so he lies around the house all day long. He's pathetic. I'd leave him today if it weren't for Tracy. I

*cry myself to sleep, thinking what I've become living with him.
When we first met, I weighed a hundred and twenty pounds. He's
such a slob, he turned me into one, too."*

*Sal nodded sympathetically while Betsy confided her secrets to a
complete stranger. When Betsy brought her back downstairs, Sal's
heart nearly felt a pang when she saw Z. attempting to clear a space
for her on their decrepit couch.*

"I've got to go," said Sal.

*"You have to stay for just a few minutes," said Betsy, and then,
"Tracy! Tracy! Wake up. A friend of your father's is here. Say
hello."*

*The girl's sad eyes drifted toward Sal. Inside them, Sal saw a
multitude of hurts and humiliations. She knew that everything Z.
and his cronies had done to Sal in junior high had been visited a
thousand times upon his daughter. The sins of the father were
brought to bear on the child. Sal suddenly felt ill, as if she might
hurl.*

She turned to Z. and said, "Great seeing you again."

*She smiled at Betsy and said, "Thank you for showing me your
lovely home."*

And then she exited the house, running to her car.

*"Wait," called Betsy. Z.'s wife hoofed across the dying lawn to
the car just as Sal locked herself inside it. The wife knocked on the
passenger-side window. Sal stomped the gas, zooming at seventy
miles an hour. Away.*

- -

While having these thoughts, I recognized them for what they
were: pure, undiluted egotistical fantasy. Building myself up
while knocking Z. down. I called Judy (friend, not

mother)—my punk rock role model in high school, who'd been just as harassed by Short Hills boys, but for different reasons—and asked, "Am I really this spiteful? Still? Shouldn't I have learned to be kindhearted and generous at some point?"

"That scumbag doesn't deserve your generosity," said Judy. "Once a shithead, always a shithead, I always say."

"That would make a lovely Hallmark card," I said.

If I did manage to get a bead on Z., I knew that the reality of making contact wouldn't be close to the fantasy. The idea of asking, "Why were you so mean to me in junior high?" terrified me. What could he possibly say to justify his cruelty? I hoped he'd stammer and beg forgiveness. I'd unleash some of my time-honed acid articulation on him. He'd probably hang up on me, but at least I'd have had my say.

After weeks of false starts, I started hunting Z. in earnest. I typed his name into a few search engines. His was a common name, the Jewish equivalent of Joe Smith. I wasn't expecting to get a direct hit on Google, and I sure didn't. I must have checked two hundred tags; none were useful. I called Liz, my lifelong friend who still lived in Short Hills, and asked her to tap into her sources for any clue to Z.'s whereabouts. She sniffed around discreetly and came back to me with two nuggets: Z. had gone to law school after college graduation, and he'd moved to a large tropical southern state. I searched that state's bar association, real estate, and police records. Nothing.

On Switchboard.com, I found several dozen listings for his name in the state. I connected to a tracker Web site that, for a fee, would provide active phone numbers and address histories for each listing. The site provided a teaser, the ages and known relatives of the listees. I eliminated all but five of the listings on age alone. Still, that got me only so far. For active phone numbers, I'd have to pay twenty-five dollars. Paying would be too easy. I was determined to find him using only my reporting skills. It'd be all the more satisfying.

A couple of the entries on my short list included a woman's name as a known relative. We'll call her U. I wondered if U. (not Betsy) was Z.'s wife's name and did a Google search for Z. and U.'s names together.

Bingo. I turned up a twenty-three-year-old *New York Times* wedding announcement. That clip provided me with U.'s maiden name—thankfully, an unusual one—and the former address of her parents in Westchester. A Switchboard .com search of that name in Westchester County turned up a listing, along with an active phone number. I dialed. A woman answered, first ring.

"Hello," I said. "I'm trying to find the parents of U."

"I'm her mother," said the woman.

I almost dropped the phone. My first call, a direct hit.

My heart pounded. Stupidly, I hadn't prepared a speech. I stammered, "My name is Val Frankel. I'm a friend of Z.'s from high school, and I'm trying to track him down . . . for a project I'm working on. I'm a journalist."

"Give me your name and number, and I'll pass it on to him," she said briskly. "Hurry up, I'm on the other line."

I gave her my info, and we hung up. My pulse was thundering in my veins. I called Liz and told her what happened. "He won't call," I said. "Why would he? He must know I hate him."

Liz said, "He'll be curious. I bet he calls tonight."

The thought made me queasy—but excited. Steve and the kids arrived home from karate, and I told them I'd found Z.'s in-laws and left my number. They knew I'd been on the hunt, searching for traces of blood in the water. Maggie was behind me all the way about confronting Z. I was her age when he started teasing me. When I told her about my past as a fat loser, she was outraged on my behalf. She seemed to crave my redemption as much as I did.

Maggie asked, "What if he doesn't call?"

"I'll phone the in-laws again in a week, and pester them every day until Z. calls to tell me to leave them alone. When I go after a source, I can be relentless. I've worn down people before, and I will again. I'm committed. I'm on a mission. I'm—"

Ring. My heart leapt into my throat, my hands shook. The caller ID display showed the name of a large tropical southern state.

I said, "It's him." Maggie ran over to me, her eyes and mouth wide open.

I pressed the TALK button. "Hello?" I asked. Casual.

"Hello, Valerie? It's Z. I heard you called my mother-in-law."

"Hello, Z. How's it going?"

"Great," he said. "Sorry about the static. I'm calling from the car."

He was that curious? He couldn't wait until he got home? "Thanks for returning the call," I said, going for gracious.

"It's so weird to hear your voice after all this time," he said.

Yeah. I remembered his voice, too, saying, "Valerie took a bite out of the moon," "She loves food," "Valerie ate the entire bakery."

"Here's the thing, Z.," I said. "I'm a writer now, and I'm working on a project about high school. I'd love to do an interview with you. See what you're doing." I'd start easy, lull him into a state of relaxation—and then go for the jugular.

"Well, I live in [medium-sized town]. I'm a financial adviser, specializing in retirement planning," he said. "I married my college sweetheart and have two sons. My older son just had his bar mitzvah."

"Your 'sweetheart'?" I said. "That's precious. I don't think I've called either of my husbands 'my sweetheart.'"

"We've been married for almost twenty-five years," he said. "She's a beautiful woman, but she spends money like crazy."

"I'm having trouble hearing you," I said.

"Static. I'm losing the signal. Why don't you call me at my office on Monday morning?" he asked.

I took his office number. I felt cold in my guts and hot on the surface of my skin. He'd been unsuspecting to a fault. He hadn't seemed to question my motive.

When I hung up, Maggie said, "Wow. You sounded like you didn't care at all."

"Really?" I asked.

"Totally."

Excellent, I thought, rubbing my hands together, à la *The Simpsons'* Mr. Burns. Nonchalance was the perfect disguise.

Over the weekend, I consulted my panel of advisers about how to handle the upcoming interview. Alison was opposed to the whole thing. "I don't understand what you hope to achieve," she said.

"I'm going to give him the golden opportunity to apologize to me," I said. "Then I'll be able to forgive him and get on with my life."

"You can't get on with your life otherwise?" she asked. "Did Z. really make your life hell, or did you give him the power to upset you? Are you seriously telling me Z. has loomed in your head as Evil Incarnate all this time? He's just some guy! He lives in friggin' [large tropical southern state]. He's a financial planner and complains that his wife spends too much money. Talk about the banality of evil. Part of letting go—which is your ultimate goal, right?—is growing up. Is it the act of a grown-up to start a fight with someone you haven't seen or spoken to in twenty-five years? If you still care about junior high, you're locked at that level of emotional development."

Rebecca had her doubts about a throw-down, too. "God knows, I love confrontation," she said. "The more confrontation the better. From what you say, though, he sounds like a loser, an easy target. Also, you might come off badly."

"How?"

"Consider flipping it," she said. "Say someone you hadn't thought about in twenty-five years called you and said, 'You know, back in junior high? You really hurt my feelings!' *Now* who's the loser?"

That made me spit my coffee laughing. I said, "You're the one who told me to eat the rat."

"You did, by calling him," said Rebecca. "You faced your fear. It's enough."

Judy (friend, not mother) was still in favor of me taking him out. "Look, you've proven that you're courageous. Posing nude? Doesn't get braver," she said. "But this isn't a test of your mettle. It's doing what needs to be done. I was there, Val. I know how much he deserves it."

Judy (mother, not friend) said, "Life is short. We all make mistakes. Don't be mean to Z."

My friend and former *Mademoiselle* colleague Daryl said, "You'll blindside him. He probably doesn't remember harassing you. If you accuse him, you might have to jog his memory about how he treated you, things he said. That would be awful!"

It seemed impossible that Z. wouldn't remember that for three years, approximately five to ten times a day, he'd either make an obnoxious gesture to me, such as puffing out his cheeks and walking like an elephant, or hurl a cutting remark, such as "fat load," "pig," "cow," or, the fantastical favorite, "beast." How could he have forgotten that he'd corralled his worshipful followers to match or best his slurs, and then rewarded them for it by doling out prized high fives in the school hallway? If I hadn't been his target, Z. and I wouldn't have had any social interaction. We had no friends or interests in common. He was a jock; I was a freak. Yet we were glued in my memory by the sticky resin of damage done. I feared Z.'s judgment in the eyes of every man I met, from junior high onward. Men judged women, harshly. That truth was imprinted on my operating system at age thirteen, the year I met Z. and his henchboys. If he remembered me—which he did—how could he not also remember what he'd done to me? He'd taken such apparent joy in cruelty, I assumed he looked back on it with nostalgic fondness—or regret, if he turned out to have a conscience. If Daryl was

right, and Z. had forgotten he'd been a huge asshole, then he
was an even *huger* asshole, which hardly seemed possible.

Steve shrugged when I asked him how I should handle
the interview. "Make the call. Just talk to him, find out what
he's like. He was a jerky kid. He's probably a jerky adult.
Confirmation of his jerkiness might be all the redemption
you need."

Monday morning, Maggie asked at breakfast if I was still going to
call Z. I said, "Yes."

"You have to tell me everything," she said, her eyes glow-
ing.

Maybe I *was* locked at the junior high level of emotional
development. Maggie, a bona fide middle schooler, was
pushing me hard to injure Z. for past insults. She wanted me
to do to Z. what she'd love to do to the popular girl who
didn't invite her to an exclusive party, or to the boy who
called her a shrimp.

"I want details," she said. "The juicier, the better."

I made the call. Not for Maggie, but for me. Blowing it
off would've been a total cop-out. Besides, I was curious
about his life. I dialed his number, my fingers trembling. I
was still undecided about whether I should demand an expla-
nation or an apology.

I understood Alison's point, that I needed to let go and
grow up, but I didn't agree that calling was childish. I was
erasing my fear by facing it, like an adult. Whether it was
right or wrong to view Z. as the symbol of my teenage woe
and lasting fear of male judgment didn't matter. That was

what he'd become in my mind, and I wanted the weight off me.

"Right on time," he said, picking up.

"Thanks for giving me your time, Z.," I replied. "As I mentioned, I'm doing preliminary interviews for a writing project. Looking back at high school. Seeing where people are now."

"Got it," he said.

"Tell me about your life."

He did. I nearly dozed off after two minutes. He told me about his fantasy football league, his yard work on the weekends, how he dotes on his children, his surprise fortieth birthday party at a cabin in the woods. He said he was in close touch with *thirty guys* from high school and rattled off names I'd completely forgotten. (When I told Rebecca about that, she said, "I guess he's still popular.") I asked if he had friends from other phases of life, and he said, "A few guys from my college soccer team." He had a law degree, but being an attorney was "too demanding," so he quit. His career was "decent." He loved his wife and kids. He was renovating his garage.

In short, he was boring as hell. The golden boy, the charismatic leader who'd seemed destined for greatness, had grown up remarkably unremarkable. He demonstrated zero imagination, ambition, curiosity. Despite the fact that I asked him dozens of personal questions, he failed to ask me a single one. Not even "Do you have kids?" which was pretty much a standard for any reunion-type conversation. Liz said curiosity would make him call me back. Wrong. He'd been motivated by vanity, I realized, not curiosity. He said he wasn't "much of a reader" and didn't follow politics "too closely." He hadn't traveled beyond predictable destinations like Paris and London. He lived in New York City for a few years after grad school, but rejected the epicenter of world culture in favor of his soulless southern state "because I hate the cold." He went on at length about his "best" pals from high school, serving up stories about going to each other's kids' bar mitzvahs, including X.'s (also a financial planner in the same state).

I started to ask questions that probed a bit deeper. About aging, relationships, regrets. He claimed to be immune to all the symptoms of the human condition. No disappointments, no regrets, he said. Finally, I broke out the big guns, a question that would put me on a direct path to his emotional core. "So, you're a married suburban financial planner with two kids," I said. "Is this the life you dreamed about?"

"I never had any dreams," he said.

"Oh, come on! When you were twenty and idealistic and had fantasies about how your life would go, about leaving a mark . . ."

"Honestly, I never had dreams about my future," he said. "I don't care about changing the world or leaving a mark. I just want to be a good friend, father, and husband, and to retire early and play golf."

"That's it?"

"That's it!" he said proudly.

I got off the phone shortly thereafter. A confrontation about our blighted past was beside the point. Why ask for a heartfelt apology from a man who had no conflicted emotions about anything he'd done in his entire life? He didn't grapple with choices. He didn't have anything to prove to the world, let alone to himself. He was content to live out his days and then fade gently, good night.

Naturally, my knee-jerk reaction was to judge him harshly for being so self-satisfied. But I couldn't muster the contempt. The person I'd held up as a monster from my formative years was just a bundle of skin, a thoughtless consumer of the earth's oxygen. Z. had chosen—gleefully—an ordinary life. And that was fine for him. It was fine for anyone.

That life would never be enough for me, though. Not to imply that I was better than him—but at least I had dreams! They defined who I was and who I wanted to be. They spurred me forward, motivated and inspired me to reach higher, prove myself, leave a mark, make an impact on the people close to me, as well as distant strangers in foreign lands. Although my choices had been predictable—college, career, marriage, kids—I'd tried to be extraordinary within (or a few steps beyond) the boundaries of convention. Being a good friend, mother, and wife was paramount. But I wanted—I needed—more.

Strivers are driven to test themselves over and over again. They don't rest on their accomplishments. Success urges them to reach higher, take bigger risks. If they fail, they pull themselves back up. Ambition is the essence of human evolution. Strivers adapt to their changing environment.

I was a striver. My environment—the body I lived in and the mind that controlled the body—was changing. I could feel it. In fact, while I was on the phone with Z., the ground shifted beneath my feet. Not because I understood him—or his past actions—better. Talking to him made me see myself more clearly in comparison.

In the days that followed, I fixated on the oddness of Z.'s having no dreams. My dreams were my road map for life. They were my goals. Without goals, I wouldn't know what to do with myself. By the end of the week, I made the important (though, in hindsight, glaringly obvious) connection between being a goal-oriented person and being a chronic dieter.

Thinness was a dream, a goal. I'd chased the dream of being a size eight, and had caught it many times, only to watch it slip away. Unlike a few of my other dreams—for example, writing a best seller that touches the hearts of millions of readers—losing weight was within my control. So, I reasoned, it was possible that, on a purely subconscious level, I'd regained weight dozens of times over thirty years *on purpose,* so that I could feel the rush, the satisfaction, of losing it again and thereby achieving my dream.

The thought was so twisted, I could hardly believe I had it. But the logic made sense. Perhaps dieting itself wasn't my compulsion. What was? Realizing a dream. The same dream, over and over again.

Objectively, I could see how this wasn't a smart life strategy. Having goals was useful, but repeating the same success/failure cycle was downright Sisyphian. And I'd been pushing the boulder up the hill, only to stand aside and let it roll back down *intentionally*!?! It was worse than Sisyphian. It was *Assholian.*

I added another vow to my ever-lengthening list.

God as my witness, I would never be Assholian again!

15

THE MOTHER LOAD, PART THREE

Talking and eating. The usual business with Mom. We were at the kitchen table in Short Hills having breakfast the morning of my reading at the temple luncheon. I was going to read excerpts from this book, about chronic dieting, silencing the Inner Bitch, and posing nude. I'd driven out to Short Hills from Brooklyn the night before and slept in my childhood bedroom, the place where I'd scribbled madly in my journal, playing the Ramones at full blast, rattling the windows and frightening the dogs.

I asked, "Who's coming, again?"

Mom recited a list of names. For charity events like this, you have to purchase "a chair" for fifty dollars or "a table" for five hundred dollars. Mom fronted five hundred dollars to reserve a whole table and then gave away or sold the seats to her friends. Some of the spots would be filled by the women who, according to Mom, had been just as relentless about their daughters' weight as Judy had been about mine.

I said, "It's so sweet that they're coming."

"Not to support you," said Mom. "To support me!"

"I'm barely mentioning you," I said.

Was that a flicker of disappointment I saw in her eyes? Probably not. I knew Mom was worried that I'd out her as an imperfect mother. She had a reputation to protect. She'd sent three kids to Dartmouth, after all. Two of us were published authors. The other had a master's in engineering. None of us were rich, alas. By Short Hills standards, Alison, Jon, and I would be considered lower class. To Mom's credit, she always cared more about our accomplishments than our salaries.

"You didn't have to a buy a table," I said. "I could have gotten you a chair for free."

"And go alone?" she asked. "*Never.*"

Mom had a peculiar quirk. Correction, Mom had *dozens* of peculiar quirks, but I was referring to one in particular. Judy had never eaten alone at a restaurant or café, nor gone to a party or function by herself. I learned this about her only last summer. We were sitting (where else?) at the kitchen table in Vermont—reading the paper, drinking the coffee— when Steve called to check in and say that he'd arrived safely at JFK (he was returning from a gig in London) and was going to grab a bite at an airport pub before cabbing home. Mom listened to my end of the conversation and then asked, "He's going to a restaurant?"

I said, "He's hungry."

Mom said, "By himself?"

"He's got a book."

Mom said, "I'd rather die than eat alone in public."

"Why?" I asked, astonished.

"When I see people alone in restaurants—even if they're reading—they look lonely and pathetic. I'd couldn't possibly let myself be seen that way," she said.

"It's official," I said. "You are insane."

"It's just how I feel," she said. The usual "I am who I am" defense.

I reached for my purse and took out my wallet. "I'll give you a hundred bucks to go to Starbucks with the *Times* crossword puzzle and sit at a table with a cup of coffee. For fifteen minutes," I said, slapping twenties on the table.

"I couldn't," said Mom.

"Two hundred."

"Not a chance."

I tore a blank check out of my book and quickly scribbled on it. Holding the check up, I said, "One-time offer: If you go to Starbucks and sit at the counter for five minutes, I will give you *one thousand dollars!*"

"Forget it," she said. "I'm sure you'd dance naked on the counter at Starbucks for half as much!"

"You making an offer?"

"Give me that," she said, taking the check out of my hand and tearing it up.

I knew she wouldn't do it (or I'd never have offered a thousand bucks). Mom could go to a park by herself (with the dogs), or sit in a movie theater, but she couldn't be seen in an *eating* establishment, or at an *eating* event, by herself. This phobia was like another layer of her skewed views about food, eating, and weight. She was in horror at the idea of being thought of as pathetic and lonely by strangers. Interesting, she was so afraid of being judged yet so extremely judgmental herself.

"I find it ironic that you assume a solo diner is pathetic, when the fact that he has the self-possession to eat alone in public proves he's more emotionally stable than you are!" I said.

"Shut up, Valerie," she said, which was her way of changing the subject.

Appearance—make that *appearances*—dominated Mom's thoughts. Being seen eating alone was a sign of weakness or failure to her. Just like having an overweight daughter.

It was setting the bar pretty low in terms of personal accomplishment, but I ate alone at restaurants often. I selfishly grabbed an hour of peace and quiet whenever I got the chance. Solitude had always been a welcomed escape. Mom? I think she had enough solitude when she was a neglected child, and had become an intensely social person to make up for lost face time. She loved to entertain, go out with friends, surround herself with family. She was chatty in the extreme. Nary a silent moment passed by; she would quickly fill it with words. She compulsively crammed empty spaces with people, dogs, furniture, and art. Judy kept herself busy, too. Always chopping, cooking, decorating, doing dog visits at hospitals, organizing, shopping. She rarely had time and quiet to be alone with her thoughts. By choice, I assumed.

Mom's deepest fears, the ones she drowned out with conversation and activity, had to be old, and sculpted sharp by the passage of time. Despite her stabs at therapy, Mom hadn't found a way to conquer her anxieties, or the will to try. She outright rejected psychopharmacology for herself, although she encouraged others to explore it. She had no intention of changing, or even considering whether change might make her happier.

Whereas I sought evolution with the fervor of a convert. This apple had fallen from the tree, rolled down the hill, and made a wild dash out of suburbia, to seed and flourish in the city. My desperate scramble out of New Jersey had been motivated by my impulse to explore—the city and my psyche. I'd been in therapy. I'd tried past-life regression, hypnosis, psychic readings, tarot readings, yoga, hallucinatory drugs, sacral-cranial therapy, energy work, reflexology, and all manner of massage. As a magazine writer, I'd road-tested colon cleansers, lip plumpers, fish oil supplements, and tiny plastic devices to strengthen the muscle tone of the vagina, among many other pills and appliances.

I'd been an intrepid explorer. I'd ventured forth and deep, emotionally speaking, but not that far geographically. Unlike my brother, a neo-Californian, I lived just twenty miles from my childhood home. I was connected to Short Hills, to my parents and the landscape. I visited often, brought the girls to see their grandparents and the dogs. There was comfort to be found in the familiar, even if the familiar had once kicked my ass.

My kicked ass and I arrived at the temple lunch on time. I recognized faces, but I couldn't remember names (see above, re: hallucinatory drug use). Although I hadn't seen some of these women for decades, many looked exactly the same. I hoped I looked half as good as my suburban contemporaries, most of them the wives of wealthy husbands and full-time moms, having quit their jobs when they got pregnant. Merely a statement of fact. I was not judging. If I had a rich husband, I'd probably work a lot less . . . actually, I probably wouldn't. I loved my job! Plus, I had those dreams. But whatever. While talking to the grown-up versions of girls I knew in high school, I flashed backward and saw their faces and hairstyles as they once were. Lauren H. (née L.) brought along a snapshot of a third-grade sleepover party. There I was, on the couch, reading a book. I looked exactly like Lucy does now. And not fat at all, btw.

Liz appeared at my side and stayed there, as she'd promised to do. Her memory was frighteningly sharp, and I needed her to feed me names and make the connections when women came over to say hello. People introduced themselves as the girl who sat next to me in junior high science class, or the friend of a friend from my brother's grade, or a kid I went to summer camp with. They mentioned the titles of my books, specific articles I'd written, TV appearances, reviews of my novels in newspapers and magazines, the Vows column on our wedding in the *Times* Styles section.

Short Hills, a small town, had produced a fair number of well-known authors. Much to my amazement, at least in this crowd, I was among them. The women treated me as if I were a teeny tiny bit famous! That felt *good*. My dress, meanwhile—the brown embroidered empire-waist creation from Banana Republic—felt *great*. In a room packed with rich housewives who considered the Short Hills Mall their daily stomping grounds, I was not a slouch. My chocolate high-heeled sandals matched my new Longchamp purse. I'd blown out my hair. My fingernails and toenails were immaculate and polished. I'd stroked on mascara and lipstick. I was passing for stylish. Stacy London was right. The feeling of being well put together was a powerful tool, an easy way to make an impression without writing or saying a word.

The speeches got under way. Liz introduced me. She gave a brief talk about how I'd always been a misfit in this town (she described it euphemistically as "marching to the beat of her own punk rock drummer"), and how I was continuing to follow my own divergent path on my search for truth. "The naked truth," she said, referring to the article in *Self* that landed me this gig. She also described me as her friend of thirty-five years. Liz had seen me at every stage, every weight. I'd seen her grow up, too, although she'd been consistently beautiful, only her hair changing over the years from Dorothy Hamill to Heidi Klum and most lengths in between. I got choked up when she read her speech. Tingle in throat. Right before I was supposed to start reading. I had to compose myself by pinching my forearm. Then I got up, was applauded by the crowd of 150 women, and started talking about the fear of being fat.

As readings go, it was very good. The women were with me for the entire half hour. During the Q&A afterward, one woman asked, "Do you think body image issues are a particular danger for our daughters in this environment?" She meant affluent suburbs.

I said, "Yes." I spoke the truth, since we were being naked about it, and listed the reasons: pursuit of status, social pressure, sky-high parental expectations, conspicuous consumption, too much free time, too much attention paid to appearances. I didn't dwell on how living in Short Hills had twisted my own body image. I'd been invited to entertain the ladies, not bite the hand. I added, "But bad body image can happen to girls anywhere, in any environment, in any kind of family." I could wind up the greatest, healthiest role model about body image on the planet, and my daughters would still have to contend with their peers, cultural pressure, the media. I said as much to the ladies.

I might've been hoping to have a big redemptive moment, along the lines of "I was a loser here twenty-five years ago, and now I'm standing in front of the microphone!" But that sentiment was irrelevant. I saw the audience as my people, women who'd struggled with body image and were worried about it on behalf of their daughters. I felt only grateful for having been asked to talk, and for being listened to.

Also, as promised, I barely mentioned Judy. Her friend Anita, seated at Judy's right at their table, was disappointed. She said, "I was all ready to jump out of my seat and shout, 'I object!'" That made me laugh.

The lunch concluded, the ladies filed out. The organizers had set up a table where I could sign and sell my books. Mom sat next to me and did the hard work of making chatter. I smiled at the buyers as best I could, but the reading had sapped my energy. Mom picked up the slack, made small talk with everyone, was charming, funny, and "up," as always. Her talk skills probably doubled my sales. Another reason to be grateful.

I asked Mom what she thought. She said, "The women loved it. They were paying attention and seemed to relate. A lot of nodding and laughing at appropriate moments."

"What did *you* think?" I asked.

She pursed her lips. "You seemed confident. I wouldn't have the courage to speak in front of a hundred and fifty people like that."

Although Mom was socially fearless—she could talk to anyone, anywhere, anytime—she shied away from the spotlight. She loved to cook and entertain, but rarely held court at her own fetes, preferring to run back and forth between the kitchen and the service tables, having bite-sized conversations with her guests along the way. I urged her to hire caterers so that she wouldn't be so busy at her own parties, and she insisted she liked to do it her way. "Her way" was to do everything, except be the center of attention. In the dozens of family celebrations we'd been to together, I'd seen her make only one toast—at my wedding with Steve, when she touchingly welcomed him into our family.

"I was surprised by some of what you said," admitted Mom as we walked to the temple parking lot. "I didn't realize you were so preoccupied with weight. I knew you went on diets, but I didn't realize you cared that much."

Visible distortion in the Force. I was dumbfounded. How could my mother be unaware of a dominant theme of my life? Either she'd been selectively blind or I hadn't told her.

Probably both. I hadn't described my diets. She didn't comment on my size fluctuations. Although weight had been the epicenter of our relationship during my adolescence, the subject had been off-limits since I started my independent life in Brooklyn. Once I was self-sufficient, I cut off uncomfortable conversations the same way she did. I'd say, "Shut up, Judy," with a warning tone, and she would. I was willing to talk to her about anything else: dating (well, not sex), my job, books in progress, then Glenn, the wedding planning, pregnancies, etc. I always went to Mom first in a crisis. No one on earth was more reliable than Judy when the chips were down. I'd turned to her for advice on practical matters big and small, parenting to gift giving. She told me the mundane details of her day-to-day life.

Although we'd exchanged millions of words over thousands of cups of coffee, how much had we revealed of our intimate lives to each other? Our conversations were light, practical, logistical. We hardly ever waded into the deeper waters of our emotions. Even during the most emotionally fraught time of my life, when Glenn was sick, Judy was my rock about practical and tactical matters. But about the feelings? My friends heard that part. I'd written articles for magazines that had exposed my soul to anonymous millions, but I hadn't really opened up, not all the way, to my mother. Mom barely knew me, I realized.

And I barely knew her. For all I hadn't shared with her, she'd shared even less with me. We didn't trust each other. On some level, I would always be fearful and defensive about her criticism. She would probably be anxious that I was holding a grudge.

We got in the car. Judy drove out of the temple parking lot, toward home. The familiar, unchanging place.

I'd been able to stop dieting for the last nine months. Would I ever stop distrusting my mom? Moreover, I wondered, would Judy ever really, truly, deeply trust me? As she said, she was who she was. She would not change. Was our relationship also set in stone? I was willing to explore unfamiliar ground, to open up to Mom. Maybe she'd open up to me. Surely *we* could evolve.

Or not. For a relationship to develop, each person in it has to hold up a mirror and look at herself closely and honestly. I was willing to gaze into the mirror and see the reflected (naked) truth, be it beautiful or terrible. Mom? Not so much.

I was going to have to accept her for who she was, and our relationship for what it was, and let sleeping fat dogs lie wheezing in the corner.

I'd asked a lot from Judy in recent months, interviewing her about her childhood, confronting her about our past. It was already July. Steve and I were back in Vermont for parents' weekend at Maggie and Lucy's sleepaway camp. At the kitchen table in Thetford, over berries and scones, I asked Judy for one more thing: to read what I'd written in this memoir.

"I'm not going to do it," she said. "You can believe what you want to believe. You can write what you want to write. But I don't have to have anything to do with it."

I asked Dad if he was going to read it, and he said, "I'm not sure."

Later, in private, Steve and I talked about Judy's response. I said, "Gave me an instant iced-over feeling."

He nodded. "It did seem a bit cold."

Frankly, I was relieved Judy would give this book a pass. Still, her rejection—hard and fast—stung. She wasn't willing or able to face the truth (my version of it), or to experience the difficult emotions that process would evoke. She might as well have wagged her index finger in my face and said, "I will *not* go there."

Thirty years from now, if Maggie and Lucy wrote memoirs that included their grievances against me, of course I'd read them. I'd be dying to read them! I'd be first in line for a peek at the inner workings of my daughters' minds, insight about their thoughts and feelings, and a sense of how they'd experienced their lives—with me and apart from me. I'd use that knowledge to better understand them, and myself, and to strengthen our relationship.

Judy would predictably buy Christmas gifts in May, be available for babysitting, have lots to say about any topic that sprang to mind. She'd be boundlessly helpful, making arrangements, giving advice, offering suggestions. I'd always fill her in on the mechanics of our lives, the comings and goings, the projects and purchases. With exciting news or in crisis, Mom would get the first phone call. As always, we'd be thisclose, and miles apart.

16

EMOTIONAL MAINTENANCE

Months of not-dieting had come to this: I was, once again, a size eight. A real eight. Not the delusional eight of cramming one's ass into stretch jeans at the Gap and declaring victory. I could walk into just about any store in New York, grab a pair of size eight pants off the rack, and button them comfortably.

I considered myself Test Subject #1. A walking (jogging) contradiction. An American paradox. In eleven months, I'd shrunk two dress sizes without dieting. The weight loss was gradual, physically painless. I had some tough moments along the way, but they were, if unsettling, ultimately constructive. Every so often, Inner Bitch would sneak a barb through my defenses, but I'd learned to squash the negative thought before it ricocheted destructively in my mind. I'd been purposefully imperfect—sometimes eating ice cream while watching TV, or lazily blowing off the gym—without crippling guilt (I'd never eradicate guilt completely; a Jew thing).

I'd admitted mistakes, flaws, and mistreatment to myself and others, which, I hoped, had made me a better, more humble person.

As far as I was concerned, my theory was now proven fact. Excess weight *was* the physical accumulation of past hurts, insults, disappointments, and resentments that, once released from the mind and soul, were freed from the body. I'd purged big-time. The ancient anger, blame, and shame were out of my system. In their place was a glut of self-awareness. I was convinced that any woman—and I do mean *any*—could melt down to her genetically predetermined true weight by (1) stopping dieting today, (2) silencing her negative inner voice, (3) forgiving everyone who'd contributed to her forming a bad body image, and (4) working out four times a week.

I haven't talked much about my exercising (just as appropriate: exorcizing). I'd go to the gym, get on a machine, sweat. The details are freaking boring and didn't fit into the emotional evolution that was far more interesting for all concerned. As it turns out, however, exe(o)rcise has been part of the emotional picture. Good body image and regular exercise have been linked in a spate of recent psych studies in the last couple of years. For a magazine article, I interviewed a grad student from Marymount University about her research. She told me she saw a bump in body image in subjects who worked out only twenty minutes three times a week. Basically, it doesn't take all that much physical effort to shape up your mind.

I didn't want to be obsessive or a perfectionist about workouts. I aimed for four gym visits a week, and pretty much hit that mark. Conventional wisdom dictates that it takes six months for any behavior, good or bad, to become a habit. I'd broken the habit barrier. Now, if I missed two days in a row, I went a little nuts.

Otherwise, I was decidedly sane. My conscience was squeaky clean about my marriage, my mom, my role model behavior for my daughters. I'd come to absolutely *love* walking into my closet and choosing from my piles and racks of superfine new threads. (God, put a blessing on Stacy London's head! She did excellent work!) Catching glimpses of myself in storefront windows used to make me cringe. Nowadays, I paused to admire.

As anyone who's been fat and been thin can tell you, thin feels better. From the moment you wake up in the morning to the second you fall asleep at night. Throughout this process, I'd wanted to stop hating the fat. But I'd also wanted to get thinner. To let go, without letting myself go. To do a reshaping above and below the neck.

So, yeah. I was where I wanted to be. You'd think I'd be ecstatic. I *was* quite relieved and energized. My load(s) had been lightened. I walked with a bouncy step, every day. And yet:

I was terrified.

Another study here, this one not so sanguine. Per national data, only 20 percent of dieters maintained a 10 percent weight loss for a year. Since I hadn't weighed myself, I had no clue what percentage I'd lost. But I did know this: In a far more personal study, conducted over thirty years, I'd regained *at least* 100 percent of the weight I'd lost in 100 percent of the diets I'd tried.

During my glittery, shimmering past periods of size-eight-dom, I'd been cocky and foolish, assuming that, since I was thin now, I'd be able to maintain. I'd overeat, blow off jogging. Then I'd step on the scale and be surprised I'd gained five pounds. I'd vow to crash diet to get back to goal weight. Never worked as planned. I'd rebel against the restriction, regain the rest of the loss, and then suffer an emotional crash. Crash diet, indeed.

This time, I knew enough about my self-destructive patterns and motivations to be righteously afraid. Add to that the huge expense of buying an all-new size eight wardrobe. I really didn't want my snazzy new duds to be my future thin clothes. And I sure as hell didn't want to shell out an additional $3,500 (and counting) to purchase a new fat wardrobe.

Even worse than that, if I were to regain, I'd slide down a shame spiral that I might not return from. The Inner Bitch would come roaring back, and she'd be very, very angry. Steve said I was perpetually "humorless and grumpy" when my weight tracked upward. If I were to gain again, I'd hate myself and be hateful to others.

Also, think of the embarrassment! I'd opened a vein here. I'd dug deep to get *out* of a hole. If I plumped up, I'd be a failure to myself, as well as to my theories. And it'd be a public failure. Along with readings and magazine articles that preached my points, I'd been holding forth about the wonders of not-dieting at dinners and parties and lunches for almost a year. What could be more humiliating than writing a memoir about conquering body image issues, only to allow them to take over my life again?

Well, actually, there was one thing worse. How about appearing on a TV reality show, dropping 122 pounds, winning a $250,000 grand prize, and then putting nearly all of the weight back on in less than a year?

It saddens me to report that Ryan Benson, the season-one winner of *The Biggest Loser,* the show that inspired my last diet, did just that. In a June 2007 *Time* magazine article, Benson said he slipped back into his preshow bad habits, and the weight came back, at lightning (heavying?) speed. Matt Hoover, winner of season two, regained fifty-three pounds of his loss just as quickly. Erik Chopin, season-three winner, regained twenty-two pounds in just a month. God bless him, I hoped Chopin wouldn't put on another ounce, but the guy owned a deli on Long Island, for Christ's sake. He was around food all day long! The one ray of hope in the *Time* article was Kelly Minner, runner-up of season one, who not only kept off the eighty pounds she lost on the show but dropped an *additional* twenty pounds. How? Minner worked out like a fiend, one to four hours *every bloody day.*

Minner was motivated by fear of her former fat. In her office, she kept a life-size photo of herself at 242 pounds. I wondered if Minner walked into her office each morning, looked at her old figure, and tasted the sweetness of her triumph, or if she recoiled at the sight, remembering her years of misery. Minner seemed like a plucky, tough woman. I'd bet she gloried in her success, as she should.

I would rather look at my neat, pretty naked photos for inspiration than at some hideous bloated shot of me at my worst. Ideally, maintenance could be a happy existence, not fraught with fear and guilt. Since my goals for the Not Diet were emotional, I figured an emotionally based maintenance plan stood a better chance of success than my useless crash diet standby.

It seemed wise to check in with Ed Abramson and Joan Chrisler, the shrinks who'd put my feet on the not-dieting path way back at the beginning of my quest. "The emotions of maintenance?" asked Ed. "Frustration comes to mind." He talked about what he sees in his patients, how they struggle with the gap between their expected miraculous life transformation and the reality that life is more or less the same, even after dropping weight. They still don't have sixteen boyfriends and a dream job and feel at ease on the beach in a bathing suit. "It's easy to blame your unhappiness on excess weight. But if the weight goes, the unhappiness might stick around," said Ed. Enter overeating, sedentary mild depression, weight re-gain. The boomerang effect is ruthlessly quick for chronic dieters. Subconsciously—hell, *consciously*—we expect the weight to creep back on. It's always happened before. It's bound to happen again.

Nonetheless, I was always stupidly surprised that my weight losses weren't permanent. I'd reduced to thinness, so didn't that make me a "thin person"? Thin people ate chocolate cake; fat people ate rice cakes. I'd convince myself that being thin made me a thin person. And then I'd relax my standards.

"'Relaxing your standards' is the language of a dieter," said Ed. "It implies all-or-nothing thinking. But you're a nondieter now. You don't have to worry about 'cheating' or 'pigging out.'" I also had the exercise habit going for me. Apparently, among people who'd lost weight and kept it off,

94 percent worked out often. Case in point: Kelly Minner, the woman who purposefully terrified herself with a giant photo of the way she used to be.

I hated the idea of using fear as a motivator for my emotional maintenance plan. I wanted to feel *less* afraid of re-gain, not more. "Good thinking," agreed Joan. "Negative emotions are the hallmarks of diet cycling. Fear, frustration, guilt, shame. They lead to lapses, and then bigger lapses. You have to stop thinking about your past history of re-gaining. What happened to you before won't happen this time. There's a big difference between those times and now."

And that was . . . ?

"You're not-dieting this time!" she said.

Exactly. If I was going to rightfully be afraid of something, Ed and Joan told me, I should worry about lapsing into old destructive habits—like dieting.

What about my nearly pathological habit of chasing the same dream over and over again? My puzzling self-sabotage bent. Logically, the way to go there was, duh, to come up with other goals. Non-weight-related goals. Of which I already had a list as long as my arm. Among them: to finish this book, run another half marathon, cook healthy and nutritious meals for the whole family every night, and take advantage of living in New York City—the museums, theaters, concert halls—more often.

Chronic dieting had exhausted my mind and time. It was oppressing. Perhaps the biggest benefit of not-dieting was the mental space I had cleared to visualize reaching other, more important goals. Joan said, "Women's minds are cluttered with all these tiny details about calories and fat grams. One of the best things a chronic dieter can do for herself is to say, 'I refuse to waste one more minute of my life on this anymore.' You might not get to the exact dress size you want, but you can throw away useless guilt and oppression. Freedom. That's what I'm talking about."

Amen, sister! We shall overcome! Among all oppressed peoples throughout history, we women hold the dubious distinction of being the only group to persecute *ourselves*. We are our own enemies. We chose the battle that we could never win. Call it the Thousand Years War. If every woman on earth were to suddenly release her fat obsession into the wind, the world would change profoundly for the better. The world around us, and the world within.

I would not let fear control my thoughts. The maintenance philosophy I developed reflected that idea. I came up with the plan during the months of summer travel. Travel had always been as much of a journey inward as outward for me. Two trips helped me create a happiness-based maintenance plan I could live with for the rest of my life, as I intended to do.

My policy had two basic tenets. I came up with the first while in San Francisco with the family.

We flew to California right after school ended, in late June. Before we left, I told everyone who'd listen about my plans to run the Golden Gate Bridge. I ran the Brooklyn Bridge often. I loved the idea of jogging across our nation's other famous bridge. It seemed a worthy goal. And since I was setting healthy new challenges for myself, as prescribed by Joan Chrisler, I was pumped. Our hotel was located miles away from the Golden Gate's footpath, not exactly convenient, but I figured I had four mornings to figure out a way to get over there via public conveyance. Steve was happy to spend a few hours alone with the kids while I did my thing. As far as eating went, I promised myself to stick to ordinary Not Diet policy, eating whatever I wanted when hungry and stopping when full.

Almost as soon as my feet touched California ground, the eating plan was out the window. I'd read a Christopher Moore novel in anticipation of our trip, and he wrote about sourdough clam chowder bowls. I mentioned the loaf-'n'-soup dish to Maggie, and she insisted on getting one first thing. Lucy, meanwhile, had heard about the Ghirardelli chocolate shop and was obsessing on a hot fudge sundae upon arrival if not sooner. Since our hotel was located at Fisherman's Wharf, mere blocks from chowder bowl central and Ghirardelli Square, the whole family was drowning in chowder and fudge within an hour of dropping off our bags.

We ate roast pork and fried rice in Chinatown. I consumed copious Boudin bread with creamy fresh butter, using it to sop up the sauce on my empty pasta plate each night. After hiking in Muir Woods, we drove up the coast in our rented convertible and stopped at a beach shack for baskets of burgers and fries. For breakfasts, we went to a bakery for ham and cheese croissants or to a diner that specialized in sourdough French toast, yet another San Francisco treat. We'd been Left Coasters for three days when I realized I hadn't eaten a vegetable or piece of fruit since we'd arrived. And I still hadn't run the Golden Gate.

While walking along the Embarcadero after a fantastic

ferry ride and an audio tour of Alcatraz (where the inmates once rioted for being served spaghetti too many nights in a row), Steve said, "Tomorrow's your last chance to do the bridge."

"Funny how it was so important before we got here," I said. "Now, I don't really care if I do it at all."

"Are you sure?" he asked. "None of that Jewish guilt?"

Honestly, none. About any of it. So I didn't run, or stop eating when full. I was on vacation! We were so busy and having too much fun to waste a single second on negative thought. The kids had finally reached the age when we could expect them to climb a mountain, eat at three-star restaurants, and walk all over town without complaint. They were fantastic, fun co-travelers, excited about our activities, making smart shopping choices, being nice to each other (a pleasant change), grateful, polite, funny. We were a tight little crew, our (almost legal) family.

The adoption paperwork was being processed. It would take a few months before Steve was their legal father, but on that trip I felt the change in status already, a stronger cohesion. We were doing so well together, and I loved the shared experiences of our adventures, including the elaborate meals and street noshing. No way was I going to take off for half a day to pursue a personal goal that seemed less and less important or meaningful.

What did matter on this trip? Our being united in happiness, gluttony, and indulgence. Guilt and obligation didn't fit into the equation. And, upon our homecoming, I realized my new habits *were* entrenched. On the eastbound flight, I started looking forward to hitting the gym and eating lighter.

My body and soul were relieved to return to exercising and green food. And I seamlessly eased back into Not Dieter and gym-goer, as if I hadn't taken the short break at all. Any weight I put on in San Francisco came off within a week of being back in Brooklyn. No harm, no foul. In fact, the break was a help. I was so damn proud of myself for reverting to good habits. The pride spurred me on.

I thought back to previous vacations, for example, our family vacation to Disney World last summer. I didn't work out or eat well then, either. But I felt guilty and crappy about it, which tainted the trip for me. My grousing probably affected Steve's and the girls' time, too. And I sure didn't seamlessly transition back to jogging and salads when we got back. On the contrary. My post-Disney eating was just as bad as it was in Orlando.

The key differences: guilt and regret, negative emotions that brought on bad patterns. In San Francisco, I felt only positive emotions, which inspired me to bounce back into good patterns. Perfectionism really is the enemy of happiness and success.

Hence, Tenet #1: **Live a little.**

Two months later, at the end of the summer, after retrieving Maggie and Lucy from camp, the girls and I flew to West Palm Beach for a short visit with Glenn's parents before school started. They lived in a South Florida retirement community. You had to be at least fifty-five to buy property on the estate, but the average age of the residents was closer to seventy. The community was built less than six years ago. It was pretty-yet-homogenous. Lots of hibiscus plants and tropical landscaping. The terra-cotta-colored houses were identical, lined up in rows on clean streets. Whenever we visited, the girls spent practically the entire time in the pool. I always brought my laptop and tried to get work done. My role there was facilitator, helping the girls and their grandparents bond.

On previous trips, I always brought along my sneakers and sports bras, and swore I'd go to the small air-conditioned gym by the pool while the kids swam. I'd never done it. Not once, in half a dozen trips. Predictably, I'd feel the usual cocktail of guilt and regret as I unpacked my unused exercise clothes upon our return. This year, I brought my jogging gear as always, but I didn't make empty promises to myself. Instead, I took action. Each morning, before breakfast, I excused myself to the in-laws, and I went to the gym.

The place was usually deserted when I arrived, despite the fact that, by eight in the morning, the lounge chairs by the pool were already filling up. The old folk get up *early* in Florida. They eat dinner at three in the afternoon, too, but I digress. A few stragglers arrived at the gym. I was the youngest person in the room by thirty years. I felt like Wonder Woman on the treadmill, next to the ladies on my right who were walking at two miles per hour and yapping about their grandchildren. I realized how pathetic that was, comparing myself to grandmas. Keeping my head down, I did my thing and left.

The next morning, another woman came into the gym. She had to be seventy, going by the folds of skin around her neck. But that was the only area of her body with loose flesh. She was a tight, taut cougar in spandex pants, a black tank top, and the fingerless gloves I'd seen on weight lifters at my gym in Brooklyn.

The biddies on the treadmill waved and said hello to the blonde in black. She returned the greeting. Then she got down to business. As I watched from the treadmill, this old lady started stacking weights onto a bar. Forty pounds on each side. After some stretching, she lay down on the bench and started pressing the dumbbells.

After twelve reps, she stretched and did it again. Then she moved around the gym like a pro, as if she'd done it thousands of times before, which, duh, she obviously had. She went on to perform feats of strength—curls, crunches, and whatnot—that a forty-year-old *man* would crow about. The whole time, this AARP pinup smiled as she moved around the equipment. She glistened with the sheen of accomplishment. She shone with an inner light of strength. I watched her go through her paces openly, awed by the bionic septuagenarian. I might've been gawking. At one point, between crunches, she winked at me.

What did the wink mean? Probably nothing. The habitual act of a friendly person. But I decided that she was trying to send me a message. A covert message, from one exerciser to another: "Be good to your body, because it's the only one you're ever going to get." The alternative? Wind up like those obese women sprawled in groaning lounge chairs who'd driven the three blocks from their houses to the pool because it was too far for them to walk.

I wanted to be that bench-pressing granny. I wanted to be her now, at forty-one. And I wanted to be her at fifty-two and sixty-two and ninety-two, should I live so long. She seemed to represent a conscious choice between (1) a healthy, strong future of thriving and surviving and (2) a slothful existence of inactivity, illness, decline, and dependence.

The choice was obvious. For me, there would be no more fooling around with weight loss and re-gain, or protracted periods of inactivity. At a certain stage in the aging process—and I was well into that—fitness shouldn't be a goal or an obsession. Fitness is life itself.

You have to love your body as a living organism, not hate it as a flawed decorative statue. Only a fool or a child would put a premium on pretty over healthy. Bad body image, I realized, was kid stuff. Mine had kicked in at eleven. I'd dragged a childhood problem into my forties.

That wink was my wake-up call. My *grow*-up call. Which brought me to Tenet #2: **Take care.**

My bad body image, a vestige of the past, was now history. My future would be devoted to strength—of character and muscle. My new role model was that iron-pumping grandma with the fingerless gloves and the frosted blond hair. When the body image demons rattled the cage, as they surely would from time to time, I'd think of her and remember that I had only one body, and one choice. To love it—or leave it. I wanted to stay around long enough to see my daughters' daughters take a big bite out of a cookie and smile with unmitigated pleasure.

So, yeah, I choose love.

AFTER

stood in front of the mirror, appraising my outfit: a pair of flat-front chinos from J.Crew, a tank top and blazer from Anthropologie. I tried on a different jacket, to see if I liked it better. Then switched to a skirt. Changed my shoes, so I had to go with a different purse. Which made my necklace seem wrong. So I sorted through my burgeoning jewelry collection to find just the right thing.

"How much longer?" asked Steve, suddenly hovering in my closet door. "I liked it better when you took five seconds to get dressed."

"Admit you'd rather be seen in public with me in a skirt and a nice jacket than in jeans and a sweatshirt," I said, fastening my necklace, five interlocking gold circles on a chain, brand-new and not cheap, a gift to myself.

"What answer will get you out of here faster?" he asked.

The girls were now on either side of Steve, wondering what was the holdup.

Maggie said, "You look so cute. I can't go out like *this,* if you're wearing *that.*" She had on the clothes she'd been in all day, cutoffs and a T-shirt. She disappeared into her room to change. Lucy, of course, was compelled to put on a fresh outfit, too.

Steve groaned, walked out of the closet, and stretched out on the bed. "I'll take a nap," he said. "Wake me when you're done."

We were going to Pete's, our usual spot, for a last summer dinner out before the start of the school year the following day. Maggie was entering the seventh grade, the year T. proclaimed me "too fat" to crush on and sealed my junior high fate. Lucy was starting the third grade, the year our pediatrician innocently called Mom's attention to my troublesome weight problem. My girls were still slender. They didn't have any serious complaints about their shapes. Bad body image could still strike them. If it did, I'd recognize the signs and steer them away from self-loathing toward comfort in their skin. I felt adequately prepared to guide them and to be a body-positive role model. I was jogging the jog, more important than talking the talk (which I was also doing, and plenty of it).

After one last look at my outfit, I turned off the closet light. Steve was pretending to snore. I knew he was faking because his real snores are much louder.

"Ready," I said, slapping his ass.

He didn't move. I was hauling back to give him another spank when he suddenly grabbed me and pulled me down on top of him.

I screamed. The girls came rushing in to see what happened. Finding us in a smoochy grapple, Maggie said, "You're disgusting."

Lucy said, "Get a room."

"We're in a room," I said.

Steve pushed me off and stood up. "Can we go now?"

After another twenty minutes of detail work (lipstick, switching purses, feeding the cats), we finally hit the street and walked the four blocks to the restaurant. I already knew what I was going to order: steak tips on a greens salad, and a vodka tonic. I'd had the same dinner at the same place dozens of times.

We sat down at our favorite table. The girls were antic, jittery about starting school again. Steve and I listened to them chatter and held hands under the table.

He leaned over to me. "Early bedtime tonight?"

"For them, or us?" I asked.

"Both."

Before I'd had a single bite, I knew this dinner would be a meal to add to my list. It heralded the ending of one season, the beginning of another. We were whole, happy, and healthy, in mind, body, and spirit. I would treasure this evening as a snapshot, an emblematic still frame from the movie of the rest of my life.

The food was good, too.

Reading Group Gold

THIN IS THE NEW HAPPY

by Valerie Frankel

About the Author

- A Conversation between Valerie Frankel and *What Not to Wear*'s Stacy London

In her Own Words

- Postscript to *Thin Is the New Happy*

Keep On Reading

- Recommended Reading
- Reading Group Questions

A Reading Group Gold Selection

For more reading group suggestions
visit www.readinggroupgold.com.

ST. MARTIN'S GRIFFIN

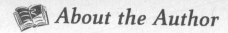

A Conversation between Valerie Frankel and *What Not to Wear*'s Stacy London

Valerie Frankel: I got dozens of e-mails from readers singing your praises. Did anyone ever mention *Thin Is the New Happy* to you?

Stacy London: God, yes. People called and wrote to me about the book. You made me a lot more sympathetic than I seem on *What Not to Wear*. The way the show is formatted, it's easy to pigeonhole me as the bad guy. In your book, you did such a good job of translating what I'm trying to say in a way that's made me sound nice and not scary at all.

VF: I never think of you as the bad guy on the show. You're funny, not scary. Clinton is a lot meaner than you!

SL: Maybe my sense of humor isn't for everyone.

VF: Are you sticking with *What Not to Wear*, despite all your fancy endorsement deals? Please say yes.

SL: I am absolutely staying with *What Not to Wear*. We've done over 260 shows, and I still think there's more to say about personal style and body image. Bad body image is among the top two or three reasons women reject or fear clothes. Experts talk about body dysmorphia—seeing yourself as having abnormal parts when, in fact, you are not abnormal—as a rare disorder. But I think we've all got a touch of it. You can certainly make yourself crazy about the demands put on women to be attractive. I've been up and down the scale my whole life. And I've blamed the pres-

> "I was a walking contradiction and identity crisis."

sure I've felt to be thin on our culture. But the more you think about it—and you, Val, really nailed this point in *TITNH*—bad body image is a symptom, but not the disease. A woman who doesn't like her body wears sweatpants to be invisible. The shell, the style itself, is evidence of an identity crisis. That's been my issue for my entire life. Who do I want to be? How am I failing myself? Am I too fat, have I gained weight? As I've gotten older, I've been better. But it's still a challenge. The more I'm in the public eye, the more it's an issue for me.

VF: **My breakthrough, in terms of style and identity, was realizing that clothes aren't superficial. Feeling special in clothes is a profound emotion. Dressing well doesn't mean I'm a lemming or a nitwit.**

SL: You do what you can. One of the issues I feel strongly about lately—and it's the angle I'm going for more on *What Not to Wear*—is how style represents a woman's emotional state. It's amazing how you can look at a wardrobe and see immediately what she is inherently insecure about. The layers of defenses she's built up are evident in her clothes. It's all there in her closet. With women especially, a terrible wardrobe tells a long story. We're finding new ways to tap into that on the show, get to the underlying reasons and forcing someone to really look at herself. Not just her clothes, but her life and her sense of self.

VF: That's exactly what you did for me. It's been two plus years since you cleaned out my closet and forced me to address my issue: Why was I

About the Author

dressing in a way that denied the essence of my personality? I was afraid of being judged by my weight, and yet I dressed in a way that made me look even larger than I really was. I was a walking contradiction and identity crisis.

SL: And now?

VF: I've spent more money on clothes in the last couple of years than I have in my entire previous life. So I'm poorer. But you know damn well that I'm a million times happier. My closet is my sanctuary. It's a world of possibilities, just as you said. Getting dressed and picking outfits makes me feel special every morning. My wardrobe and personality match—or, as you say on *What Not to Wear*, they "go." It's the difference between feeling out of whack versus being in sync every minute of every day.

SL: Another life saved.

VF: Amen, sister.

Want to know what Stacy thinks about the personal style of a famous TV talk show host?

What does she think about men and body image?

What would Joan Rivers say?

Visit www.readinggroupgold.com to read more!

"[My hope is] that all of the women who wrote to me have managed to stop the insanity of dieting."

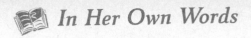

Postscript to *Thin Is the New Happy*

It's been eight months since the hardcover publication of *Thin Is the New Happy*. Eight fabulous months of bathing in the warmth of acknowledgement and camaraderie. Along with dozens of kvell-worthy reviews (*TITNH* was my nineteenth book—and the first to be reviewed in *The New York Times*), I received hundreds of e-mails from readers who found themselves in my story, got it, totally related to my experiences. Some had fatphobic mothers and found comfort in knowing they weren't alone. Some were fatphobic mothers who were desperate to get a grip on themselves or turn their daughters into, well, me. Fellow diet addicts vowed to try the not-diet. The word "hope" came up a lot, as in, "You give me hope I can conquer my own body-image demons." My fondest hope is that all of the women who wrote to me have managed to stop the insanity of dieting and have silenced their inner bitches once and for all.

Of course, you can't please all the women, all the time. Some readers found my story to be puny, banal, "ordinary" (to that reviewer, I ask, "Is it ordinary to become a widow at 35?"). One angry e-mailer called me an "East Coast snob." I am guilty of being a New Yorker. I'll take "vaguely misanthropic." But snob? I've seen too many of the real thing to accept that hit. An Amazon reviewer accused me of "self-loathing," and said I was desperately in need of intensive psychotherapy. Hmmm, my self-loathing was kinda the point of writing the book. I'm much better now, or didn't she read that far?

The *New York Post*'s Page Six gossip column
covered *TITNH*, giving it several paragraphs in
an item titled "Mag Editor Dopes to Stay Thin"
about my cocaine use in the early 1990s at
Mademoiselle. Ancient history to some, breaking
news to others. The Page Six item was picked up
by American Web sites galore, including *New York*
magazine, *The Huffington Post, Jezebel,* and *Jossip.*
The blog entries caught the eye of producers
at *Entertainment Tonight* and *The Tyra Banks
Show*. (Tyra, despite what you might've heard, is
not-a-bitch. The day I taped her show, she was
friendly and smiley, and agreed with the not-diet
philosophy completely. I liked her.) *TITNH* was
suddenly abuzz.

Surreally, the story of my lifelong struggle with
body image jumped across the Atlantic Ocean.
Two London newspapers—*The Daily Mail* and
The Observer—ran excerpts, and reprinted my
naked photos along with the text. One morning,
I received an urgent e-mail from a British TV
producer asking for permission to show my nudie
pix on his program, a British version of *The View*,
as a launch point for the hosts to chat about body
image. By the time I replied ("er, okay, I guess"),
they'd already broadcast a slideshow of quivering,
unclothed me, and had a hearty discussion about
my "bravery." After England, *TITNH* traveled
around the world, from Italy and Spain to
Australia and South Africa.

Attention memoirists: If you wish to get publicity
for your book, display your naked flesh like wall-
paper in a foreign country.

I'm recounting the wildfire of media attention for

*"My dream
as a writer has
always been . . .
for my ideas and
experiences to
touch women's
lives"*

TITNH not to brag (although, damn, that was exciting!) but to marvel at how profoundly bad body image affects the lives of women all over the globe. My (puny, banal, ordinary, self-loathing) story rang distinct and distant bells from Dublin to Johannesburg. As I mentioned in *TITNH*, my dream as a writer has always been to make an impact on readers near and far, for my ideas and experiences to touch women's lives. Thanks to *TITNH*, I've reached people and been accepted into sympathetic hearts and expansive minds. Not surprisingly, *TITNH* was the first time I'd really put myself out there in print, complete honesty, no holding back about my deepest insecurities.

As gratifying as it has been to connect with readers down the block and across the planet, the book release has caused some trouble here at home. At store signings, book fairs, clubs, and events, one of the most commonly asked questions is: "Has your mother read the book, and what does she think of it?"

My mom has not read a word of the book, nor any of the reviews. You'll recall, when I asked her to read the manuscript, she said she wanted nothing to do with it. Judy has kept her word. She (and my father) pretend *TITNH* doesn't exist. That has been a challenge for Mom, especially when the ladies of Short Hills approach her at the Kings supermarket to say, "How could Valerie do that to you?"

"My friends are outraged on my behalf," said Mom at the time. "You have no idea how hard this is for me."

After an initial flare of resentment ("Since you haven't read the book, you have no idea how hard you made my adolescence," I thought), the guilt settled in. I didn't intend to embarrass Judy in front of her friends, or hold her up as a bad parent. As I said repeatedly in *TITNH*, Judy was a fine mother, except for her obsession about weight. She freely admits she was obsessed. To some extent, she's proud of it. Many of her friends treated their daughters the same way. My great sin was writing about it. I exposed the suburban secret abuse of fatphobic mothers, called them to the empty table, and that was a break from the unspoken rules of discretion and dignity.

> "I haven't dieted since the day I started to write [this book]."

Judy feels betrayed. I am sorry about that. According to my friends, my mom's portrayal in *TITNH* was fair. Another generational divide? Mom took her pain like a trooper and kept her trap shut. I come from the heart-on-sleeve, flapping lips era, although it took thirty years of mustering courage to confront Mom about her treatment of me and write about it.

I'll finish up my postscript with the most e-mailed and asked question from readers and book club members: "Are you still not dieting?"

I am a devotee of not-dieting. I haven't dieted since the day I started to write *TITNH*, nearly three years ago. In all honesty, my weight has fluctuated within a small range. I can't say how many pounds up and down since I don't weigh myself (a HUGE relief, meanwhile). If I had to guess, I'd say I've gone up maybe seven pounds max. But then my fabulous clothes start to feel

tight, and it breaks my heart not to wear a favorite jacket or pair of pants. Instead of getting depressed, I just increase my workouts. I jog longer, and/or add an extra gym visit to the week. I cut back on sugar—if I'd been having frozen yogurt every night, I limit it to every other night, for example. A couple of weeks later, my clothes fit again, and I'm extra happy because, although my size fluctuated slightly, my mood remained the same. I have become an emotionally stable woman, at least about weight.

Does this mean my life is perfect? I wish! I'm still plenty neurotic about other bêtes—money, my husband's beer consumption, epidemic brattiness among the neighborhood kids, my shaky professional standing, the rudeness of cell-phoning assholes in movie theaters, my own shallowness and impatience as a mother, wife, and human being (all of which I'll contend with in my next memoir for St. Martin's, *It's Hard Not to Hate You*). But, as of this writing on May 1, 2009—and, I firmly believe, the rest of my life, however long it might be—I've got body image beat.

Moving along . . .

What do Valerie's daughters think of her book?

How did her husband handle all the publicity?

What ever happened to X., Y., and Z.?

Visit www.readinggroupgold.com
to get ALL the updates!

📖 Recommended Reading

I read widely, jumping genres, fiction, nonfiction, graphic novels, pretty much anything I can get my hands on. I love so many books, it's impossible to make a list. Instead, I'll recommend some of my favorite authors:

Christopher Moore, especially *Fool, You Suck,* and *A Dirty Job*. Many readers of *Thin Is the New Happy* have commented on my sense of humor. Moore's books make me LOFL (I put in the F for fucking). So, if you are looking for amusing, ribald, and clever novels—sex, foul language, supernatural beings, and chock-o-block human emotions—get Moore.

Lindsey Davis. For historical mystery fans, I love Davis's sleuth series set in ancient *Rome*. Her main character, Marcus Falco, is as sexy, charming, and fearless as the best romance-novel hero, plus he's always wearing a toga or tunic for easy access. This series is EIGHTEEN novels strong. I've read 'em all. Loved 'em all. I once corresponded with Davis (slavishly devoted fan drivel), and she was very nice.

Jonathan Kellerman. In a psychological thriller, what better main character than a shrink? Alex Delaware, Kellerman's finest creation, is smart, sympathetic, and erudite, with a voyeuristic dark side that I, for one, find humanizing and appealing. Everything I know of Los Angeles comes from Kellerman novels. Which means LA is populated exclusively with serial murders, sexual predators, and killer cultists. Never a dull moment.

Stephanie Laurens. For Regency romance (and, honestly, is there any other kind???), I get all the twitching, throbbing, heavy-breathing satisfaction

I can stand from Laurens. She supplies ruched nipples, quivering thighs, and shattering climaxes galore, as well as period details and a hoof-clomping, canter-paced plots.

Christopher Buckley. The modern satirist extraordinaire. His most famous novel is *Thank You for Smoking* but I also recommend *Boomsday* and *Supreme Courtship*. Buckley has the rare gift of clairvoyance. His novels come out and then, soon after, real world events unfold uncannily as he'd portrayed them in his books.

Mark Bittman. What, you don't sit down and read cookbooks? What's wrong with you? The *New York Times* columnist is my foodie idol. In *How to Cook Everything*, he makes any recipe seem easy, even the really freaking hard ones. No wonder he calls himself "The Minimalist." I can't cook without him. I feel like I know him. I wish I could meet him! Mark Bittman, if you're reading this, CALL ME!

John Twelve Hawkes. In the sci-fi fantasy category, I love the intense, serious, and creepy Dark River series, about a secret society of sword-wielding Harlequins who live off the grid and thwart the machinations of their ancient enemies. The characters go on trips to hell-like other worlds, such as the land of the hungry ghosts where everyone is starving, but there is nothing to eat (a.k.a. my nightmare). Twelve Hawkes (not his real name) lives off the grid himself. His location and identity are mysteries to all but his agent. Knowing that adds a sharp edge of paranoia to his already disturbing vision of our future.

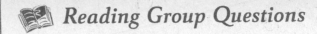

1. A show of hands: Is anyone on a diet right now? Who has been on a diet during the past year? What kind of success have you had trying to lose weight?

2. Valerie Frankel begins her book by sharing a series of dieting metaphors. A drug addiction. A gambling addiction. The five stages of grief. Do you have any of your own you'd like to add?

3. Did you find the author's tales of chronic dieting humorous or sad? Empowering or self-defeating? Discuss the issues of beauty, body image, and self-acceptance that are raised in *Thin Is the New Happy*. Does the book cover these issues in a unique way? How are they typically discussed—and portrayed—in mainstream American culture?

4. Valerie decided to tackle her dieting obsession once and for all around the time her daughters were reaching puberty. In what ways do you think Valerie's attitudes about her own body changed once she became a mother? Do you think weight is a different issue for children than it is for adults? How?

5. In her postscript, the author mentions that her mother, Judy, never read *Thin Is the New Happy*. Judy's friends did, however—and were outraged on her behalf. What do you think of Valerie's portrayal of Judy in this memoir? Was it fair and balanced? Did Judy emerge as a sympathetic character . . . or a bad mother? And what do you think of Judy now?

6. "I am a connoisseur of insult and criticism," writes the author. "My ears prick up to catch the slightest intonations, the smallest hint of negativity, even in a seemingly benign comment." Another show of hands: Who in the group can recall at least one episode of childhood taunting? (Some of you may want to share your stories.) How can "innocent" teasing have a lifelong effect on one's sense of self?

7. Take a moment to talk about the men, past and present, in Valerie's life. How did they view her? Were they able to see her for who she is on the inside? Also, how did you react when her husband told her: "I adore every inch of your body. And it'd be even better if you could get rid of the stomach." In what ways did this one remark unleash a lifetime of bad feelings Valerie had about her weight? How would you feel in her shoes—or his?

8. After reading the author Q&A in this Reading Group Gold guide, do you agree with Stacy London that bad body image is a symptom, not a disease? Which was it for Valerie? Why?

9. Valerie decided that, with this book, she would finally tell the "naked truth" about her weight obsession. With this in mind, have a look at one of Valerie's nude *Self* magazine photographs (go to: http://origin.www.self.com/health/2007/06/ how-nude-portraits-can-help-self-image). What do you think, now that you've seen it? Does it make you think any differently about the author's journey? How?